To Colin, 20
Hope you enjoy this
book about dinosaurs.
This was one of Uncle
Nicks favorite books
when he was about your
age. Love you,
Mom Mom
& xoxo

DINOSAURS
of the Land, Sea and Air

MODERN PUBLISHING
A Division of Unisystems, Inc.
New York, New York   10022

Printed in Singapore

Introduction

Think of the earth as a big house. Like your house or apartment. You and your family are the owners, or the tenants. On Earth, we the human race, are those tenants. Now stop and think some more. Perhaps you and your family were not the first people to live in your house or apartment, just as humans are not the first living things to inhabit the earth.

Prepare to meet the previous tenants of the planet earth...the dinosaurs. Sixty-five million years before the first human walked the earth, this amazingly diverse and fascinating group of creatures called it their home.

Huge creatures that caused the earth to tremble beneath their feet. Small creatures that flew through the air on leathery wings. Large bull-like monsters with huge horns on their heads. And ferocious meat-eating predators that stalked the world in search of a meal that they could catch. Ever since scientists first discovered the fossils of these creatures, people have been fascinated by the way they looked, lived, and eventually disappeared in a sudden, and still unexplained, manner.

This book, and its companion volume, *Dinosaurs and Prehistoric Creatures*, offer a unique look at the everyday life of these amazing beings. Travel back in time and learn how dinosaurs searched for food, fled from predators, protected their young, and looked for shelter. In addition to entertaining stories and bright, colorful artwork, these books contain fact and information sections and extensive glossaries which provide further information about the dinosaurs and their very different "world."

Step into this "time machine" and prepare to meet the former inhabitants of your neighborhood, city, or town. Remember—during this journey back in time *we* are the guests, peeking in on life one hundred million years ago.

Table of Contents

Diplodocus

Pteranodon

Woolly Mammoth

Chapter One
Allosaurus

Written by Ron Wilson
Illustrated by Doreen Edwards

Allosaurus

Hypsilophodon

Ichthyosaurus

The old Allosaurus could not move as quickly as she used to. Finding food was not as easy as it had been in the past. There were also more of her own kind on the lookout for large creatures to kill and eat.

Wind and rain lashed the countryside. So heavy was the rain that the old Allosaurus had difficulty in seeing where she was going.

Suddenly the wind changed direction. As it did so, it increased in strength. The rain turned to hail. The large hailstones made the old dinosaur's eyes water. She held her head down.

At the onset of the storm most of the other creatures had taken shelter. The young Archaeopteryx had climbed into the nearest trees. Diplodocus had sought the shelter of a thicket.

The old Allosaurus was so hungry that she plodded on her way. She could not see where she was going. Head down to avoid the hailstones, she moved forward. She was stopped in her tracks as she walked headlong into a tree. Her massive form made the whole trunk tremble. Up in a fork of the tree an Archaeopteryx was disturbed and clung on tightly.

The storm was short-lived. The black clouds had
gone, and in their place bright sunshine flooded the
earth. The old Allosaurus felt better. Already other
creatures had come out from their sheltering places.
They were on the move again.

It was a long time since Allosaurus had had a good meal. She had taken some lizards and small mammals. However, these weren't enough to satisfy her hunger and keep her going.

Her belly ached from lack of food. The old creature looked around her. She saw a Diplodocus feeding in the distance. There was a Stegosaurus close by. She even noticed a Brontosaurus emerging from behind a large cycad.

The dinosaur paused for a moment. She knew from past experience that Diplodocus might be easier to attack than Brontosaurus. She certainly wanted to avoid the Stegosaurus.

She had made up her mind. Allosaurus moved off slowly at first, but as the pangs of hunger increased she hastened her steps just a little. Allosaurus saw the Diplodocus move away as it fed. Stegosaurus was now much nearer. Yet, Stegosaurus with its armor plating would be more difficult to attack. The old Allosaurus realized that the creature would be too strong for her.

Allosaurus decided to leave the Stegosaurus to its food-hunting activities. She changed direction, hoping to approach the Diplodocus without being seen. There was plenty of cover from nearby trees and bushes. Allosaurus made for these.

She kept the Diplodocus in view. As she approached she caught sight of a Brontosaurus which was even closer. She changed course. The Brontosaurus was too busy browsing to notice. As Allosaurus trundled on she walked over several tree trunks which had fallen in the high winds. The sound of her feet crashing into them disturbed an Archaeopteryx. It let out a warning call. This was picked up by the other Archaeopteryx on the ground and in the trees.

Both Diplodocus and Brontosaurus heard the alarm cries. They looked up from their feeding. They both saw the Allosaurus approaching and made off in opposite directions.

Diplodocus moved off quickly. In her haste to
avoid the approaching Allosaurus it had not seen
another Allosaurus hiding behind a cycad. It was too
late. Diplodocus tried to avoid it. Within seconds the
Allosaurus had spotted Diplodocus. It moved forward
ready for the kill. Diplodocus had no chance against
this vicious creature. It struggled, but in spite of its
great strength, its efforts were in vain. The Allosaurus
had it firmly in its grip.

The old Allosaurus's hunger pangs were extremely great now. The smell of fresh flesh was too much to ignore. She continued to move towards the feeding Allosaurus and the dead Diplodocus.

She was still some way from the scene when the feeding Allosaurus let out a warning call. The old creature decided not to try her luck and turned away. As she did so she spotted an Archaeopteryx quietly feeding on insects close by.

There was little flesh on an Archaeopteryx, but anything would help to cure the hunger pangs. Allosaurus approached slowly. Within reach of Archaeopteryx it pounced. But the old creature was not quick enough. The bird escaped and climbed up the short trunk of a nearby tree.

Allosaurus went towards the tree. The old
dinosaur put its front feet onto the trunk of the tree.
Archaeopteryx was just out of reach. The frightened
bird spread its wings and glided gently down to earth.
It ran for cover as quickly as its legs would carry it.

Turning round the Allosaurus noticed that the
Brontosaurus which it had spotted earlier was now
feeding again. She decided to approach it. There was
plenty of cover from the cycads. Allosaurus was very
cautious. So great was her hunger that she must feed
soon if she was to survive.

The Brontosaurus was feeding close to a tree. Allosaurus was making slow progress. She paused. Brontosaurus was almost within reach. Eager to get a meal, Allosaurus made a sudden lunge at the other dinosaur. She missed, and Brontosaurus ran off into the distance. As it went it bellowed a warning to the other creatures. They quickly scattered in all directions.

Allosaurus had little energy left. She sank to the ground with exhaustion. She was not sure whether she would be able to get up again. Food had been scarce for some time now. She had had to compete for it with the other more agile flesh-eaters. Now she was not sure what to do. Allosaurus rested for a while. Then she tried to get up. She couldn't make it. Already she had been spotted by other creatures eager for a meal.

A young Allosaurus approached. The old creature shouted a warning which meant 'stay away'. At the same time she tried again to get up. She managed to raise herself onto two feet, but sank back to the ground again.

Realizing that the old creature was not going to make it, the young Allosaurus pounced. It sank its clawed talons into the back of the weak Allosaurus. Huge fangs tore at the flesh. The old creature shrieked in pain. Within minutes another Allosaurus had arrived on the scene.

The old dinosaur was unable to fight, and within minutes she was dead. Quickly the two Allosaurus tore huge chunks of flesh from the body of the dead creature.

Several Ornitholestes had been hiding in bushes nearby. They had been waiting for such a moment. They dashed out, grabbed small pieces of meat in their jaws. They quickly ran back for cover. The Allosaurus were too busy to see them.

Soon there was little of the old Allosaurus left. Several large bones littered the ground as the well-fed younger Allosaurus ambled off into the distance, their hunger satisfied for another day.

Rhamphorhynchus

Pteranodon

Pterodactyl

Ankylosaurus

Dimetrodon

Iguanodon

Tricondon

Chapter Two

Archaeopteryx

Written by Rupert Oliver
Illustrated by Bernard Long

Archaeopteryx

Ichthyosaurus

Plesiosaurus

Deinonychus

Nothosaurus

Archaeopteryx woke from her sleep and stretched her wings. She had been asleep since the previous evening and felt rested and full of energy. She moved from the nook in which she had been sleeping and climbed up the tree trunk. Using her clawed hands and feet, Archaeopteryx was able to scramble up the smooth tree trunk.

Archaeopteryx was hungry so she began looking for something to eat. She could not see anything, so she climbed higher up the tree. From her new position Archaeopteryx looked down on the branches below. On the upper side of one of these branches was a lizard, perhaps that would make a tasty meal.

Carefully, Archaeopteryx shifted her position, trying not to disturb the lizard. To land close to the lizard, Archaeopteryx would have to launch herself properly. Once she was airborne, Archaeopteryx could not change direction very easily. She was a very awkward flyer. She would have to time the glide down perfectly.

At last Archaeopteryx was satisfied with her position. She spread her feathered wings wide and leaped into the air. Suddenly the lizard saw Archaeopteryx above it. In fear the lizard began to run away, but it was too late. Archaeopteryx landed just inches from the lizard. In a flash she had snapped the lizard up with her sharp teeth.

Archaeopteryx held the lizard beneath her feet. She bit chunks off the reptile and swallowed them whole. Archaeopteryx could hear heavy footsteps on the ground far below, but she did not take any notice. She was about halfway through her meal when a loud rustling among the leaves startled her. Something large was moving among the branches. Anxiously, Archaeopteryx looked round but the noise had stopped. Perhaps it had only been the wind.

Then an enormous shape pushed through the leaves towards Archaeopteryx. It was larger than the whole of Archaeopteryx. Archaeopteryx was suddenly very frightened. She could only think of one thing to do. She leaped from the branch and spread her wings.

Archaeopteryx fluttered down through the air.
As she glided she looked round. The head that had
startled her so much belonged to an enormous
Pelorosaurus. The giant dinosaur was munching
away at the leaves, using its long neck to reach the
upper branches.

Archaeopteryx reached the ground safe and sound. The Pelorosaurus was a plant-eater and would not bother Archaeopteryx. She scampered into the bushes to avoid the feet of the dinosaur.

Then Archaeopteryx heard other footsteps approaching. They sounded lighter than those of Pelorosaurus, perhaps they belonged to a smaller dinosaur. Suddenly a ferocious Megalosaurus appeared from the undergrowth. The Pelorosaurus saw the mighty hunter and gave a bellow of fear. The huge Pelorosaurus lumbered off through the trees with the powerful Megalosaurus chasing close behind.

When the large dinosaur had gone, Archaeopteryx crept out of the bushes and moved on.

A large, colorful butterfly flew past Archaeopteryx. Archaeopteryx was still hungry and a juicy butterfly would be very tasty. The butterfly flitted on through the bushes. Archaeopteryx stood high on her long legs and scampered after it. Keeping the brightly colored insect in sight, Archaeopteryx pushed through the bushes. Before long she had caught up with the insect. Archaeopteryx leaped high into the air and caught the butterfly in her jaws.

As she crunched the butterfly in her jaws Archaeopteryx turned her head. Not far away the bushes thinned out. Archaeopteryx could smell water. She crept through the bushes looking for a drink.

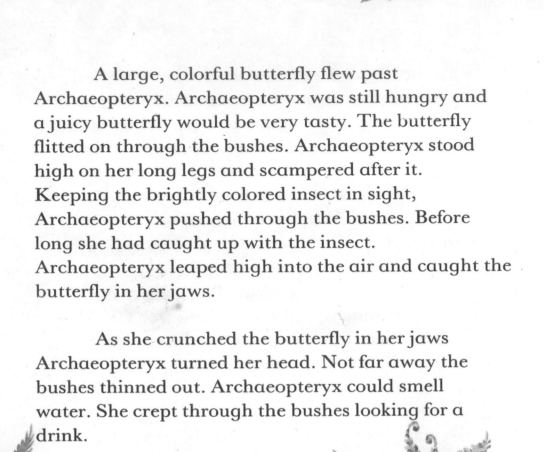

Archaeopteryx found
herself on a river bank. It was a broad river with wide
banks. The sudden glare of sunlight made
Archaeopteryx blink, but she soon saw that the
riverbanks were crowded with all sorts of animals.

Not far from where she stood a large crocodile
lay half in the water. It was basking in the sunlight
after eating a good meal. Wading in the shallows
were a pair of Elaphrosaurs. Suddenly one of the
Elaphrosaurs plunged its head into the water. When
it came up, Archaeopteryx could see that the
Elaphrosaurus had a fish in its jaw.

A sudden flurry of movement on the bank
made Archaeopteryx very nervous. Two male
Dryosaurs were fighting. Nearby a female
Dryosaurus watched the fight. Archaeopteryx
watched as the males kicked each other. Finally, one
stopped fighting and moved away. The winner
strutted over to the female and moved off with her. It
was the breeding season and the fight had decided
which was the dominant male. Then something more
interesting caught Archaeopteryx's eye.

Not far away was a dead Alocodon. It looked
as if a larger dinosaur had killed the small
plant-eater. Part of the Alocodon had already been
eaten, but there was enough meat left for
Archaeopteryx.

Cautiously Archaeopteryx approached.
Perhaps the hunter that had killed Alocodon was still
nearby. Archaeopteryx looked round carefully, but
there was nothing in sight. She began to pull at the
carcass and was soon enjoying a good meal.
Archaeopteryx had just bitten off a juicy piece of
meat when a Compsognathus arrived. The small
dinosaur wanted the piece of meat that
Archaeopteryx had. The two began to squabble over
it. Archaeopteryx was trying to hold on to it and
Compsognathus was trying to snatch it away.

It was then that Archaeopteryx realized another dinosaur was nearby. Running towards Archaeopteryx and the Compsognathus was a Teinurosaurus. It was the Teinurosaurus that had killed the Alocodon and it was coming to protect its food.

Archaeopteryx knew that if the Teinurosaurus caught her she might end up as another meal, so she ran off as fast as she could. Archaeopteryx's legs could cover ground very quickly, but Teinurosaurus could run even faster. The large dinosaur began to catch up with Archaeopteryx. There was only one chance of escape for Archaeopteryx and she took it. She took a running jump at a huge tree trunk. Archaeopteryx grabbed hold of the bark and quickly scrambled up the tree. She could feel Teinurosaurus just behind her, but the large dinosaur could not climb trees and Archaeopteryx was safe.

The Teinurosaurus glared angrily up at
Archaeopteryx, but it could not reach her so it went
away. It was beginning to get dark now and
Archaeopteryx was tired. She climbed further up the
tree. Soon she found a comfortable fork in the tree
and settled down to sleep for the night. As she rested
a Camptosaurus arrived and began to browse on the
leaves. The sun slowly sank lower in the sky and
Archaeopteryx fell asleep.

Brontosaurus
(Apatosaurus)

Pteranodon

Cetiosaur

Dimetrodon

Iguanodon

Stegosaurus

Chapter Three
Brontosaurus

Written by Angela Sheehan
Illustrated by Colin Newman

Tyrannosaurus

Triceratops

Parasaurolophus

Ornithomimus

Ankylosaurus

The river was almost dry. There was barely enough water left to cover the crocodiles. Even the spiky horsetails that used to grow thick and fast along the water's edge, were brown and wilted. For days and days there had been no rain.

The young Brontosaurus wallowed in the mud. There was not even enough fresh water to quench his thirst, but the mud cooled his hide. After a while he heaved his great body out of the murky stream and clambered up the bank. The mud caked on his skin dried hard in the baking sun.

The huge animal lumbered off to catch up with his herd. He could hear them bellowing in a maidenhair grove not far off. By the time he reached them the trees were almost bare. The hungry animals had eaten every leaf. Brontosaurus chewed the hard stems, hardly tasting their sap. Soon the sun would go down and the herd would sleep in the grove.

Brontosaurus was too hungry to sleep through the night. He woke often and listened to the calls of the prowling meat-eaters and the screeches of the pterosaurs.

In the morning, the brontosaur herd moved on. They passed a herd of stegosaurs cropping the remains of ferns that not long before had been green and fresh. Now the land was hard and dusty. The scanty patches of plants were almost as brown as the dry soil.

The sun rose high and the herd moved more slowly. They came to a waterhole where they often rested at midday. But it was dry. The trees around it were scorched and wilting. Once more the animals ate what little they could find, then moved on.

As they walked, they passed the skeleton of a dinosaur that had died in the drought. The scavenger Ornitholestes picked the last of the thin flesh from its bones. The brontosaurs picked the last of the leaves from the nearby trees and continued on their way.

Slowly the older animals in the herd began to lag behind. With so little food, they were too tired to walk. The young Brontosaurus also lagged behind, but not because he was weak.

One of the females in the herd was ready to mate. She moved more and more slowly, allowing the others to get far ahead. Only the young male stayed behind with her. The two animals walked side by side. The male roared gently at the female and rubbed her neck with his own. Then after a while they mated.

The sun was sinking now and the two animals were far from the herd. So they found a sheltered spot where there was just enough greenery for them to eat. Then they went to sleep.

The next morning Brontosaurus and his mate hurried after the others. They moved as fast as they could towards the forest. When they were almost within reach of the trees, they heard a frightful roar and a bellowing noise.

Standing as still as they could, they watched an Allosaurus bearing down on one of the old males from their herd. In his youth no Allosaurus would have been a match for him. But now the animal was too old and weak, and the great flesh-eater was savage with hunger. Brontosaurus and his mate saw its claws rip through the old animal's hide and its rasping teeth dig deep into the wound. With a bellow of pain, the old dinosaur sank dead to the ground. Allosaurus gorged. Now it was safe for the two younger animals to pass by.

By the time Brontosaurus and his mate reached
the forest, the others had moved into its depths,
munching the leaves as they went. The two animals
ate and ate and ate as they followed them. For the
first time in days they had enough to eat, and the
trees sheltered them from the sun. They lazed for a
while in the shade and then moved on. Ahead of them
they could hear the bellows of the well-fed herd. By
nightfall they had almost caught up with them.

Then suddenly out of the sky came a great
flash of light and a mighty rumble. All the animals
bellowed and roared in terror. The birds took to flight
and the dinosaurs ran. The two brontosaurs charged
through the trees, crashing against the trunks and
trampling the dry undergrowth. When they stopped,
there was silence. The silence lasted a few moments.
Then the dreadful light and sound came again,
followed once more by stillness.

The two animals waited. After a while they heard a new sound, crackling and roaring. The wind carried a strange, frightening smell. All the animals were on the move. Huge flesh-eaters headed the charge, followed by small nimble dinosaurs and scampering mammals. Lizards darted from their hiding places and pterosaurs took to the air. Brontosaurus and his mate galloped along with the others in their panic.

The whole forest was on fire. Flames and sparks, fanned by the wind, leapt from the burning branches. The animals ran and ran and ran. The flames licked along behind them, eating up the ferns and the cycads. Smoke blocked out the light of the moon. The forest was lit only by the giant red flames.

Brontosaurus and his mate ran until they could almost run no more. At last they came to an outcrop of bare rock. They scrambled up the steep cliff face, joining the other animals that had fled there from the fire. They clambered from ledge to ledge, not knowing where to go.

But the blaze could not reach them. The rocks were bare. There was nothing to burn. So they were safe. All night the fire raged below them. They watched and waited.

By morning there was nothing left of the forest but bare, blackened tree trunks standing in a layer of ash. The animals picked their way down the cliffs to the level ground, and went on their way.

As they lumbered over the rocks, Brontosaurus and his mate came upon the rest of their herd. They too had fled from the fire, but they were all safe. Together now, they moved across the plain, searching for trees to eat, as the other animals searched for ferns on the ground, or hunted their prey.

Brontosaurus soon grew hot and tired again. There were no trees, and the only pool they found was almost dry. By evening they had still found nothing to eat or drink.

Then suddenly the same light flashed that had
flashed the night before and the same rumbling
followed. But this time, instead of fire, the animals felt
soft, cool drops of water on their hides. The clouds
opened and rain poured from the sky. Great drops
splashed on to the ground and soon rivers of water
roared among the stones. Within minutes the empty
waterhole was filled. Brontosaurus and his mate
trampled in the pool and sucked up the cool water.

From then on it rained every day. The dusty ground sprang to life. Ranks of ferns grew up and the trees sprouted new leaves. The land grew green almost overnight. The brontosaur herd was able to stay where it was.

Brontosaurus spent each new day trundling
about munching first one tree, then another. His mate,
too, ate well. Later in the year she laid her eggs. And
before the dry season came again young brontosaurs
hatched from the eggs.

Dimorphodon

Brachiosaurus

Dilophosaurus

Lystrosaurus

Rutiodon

70

Chapter Four

Chasmosaurus

Written by Rupert Oliver
Illustrated by Bernard Long

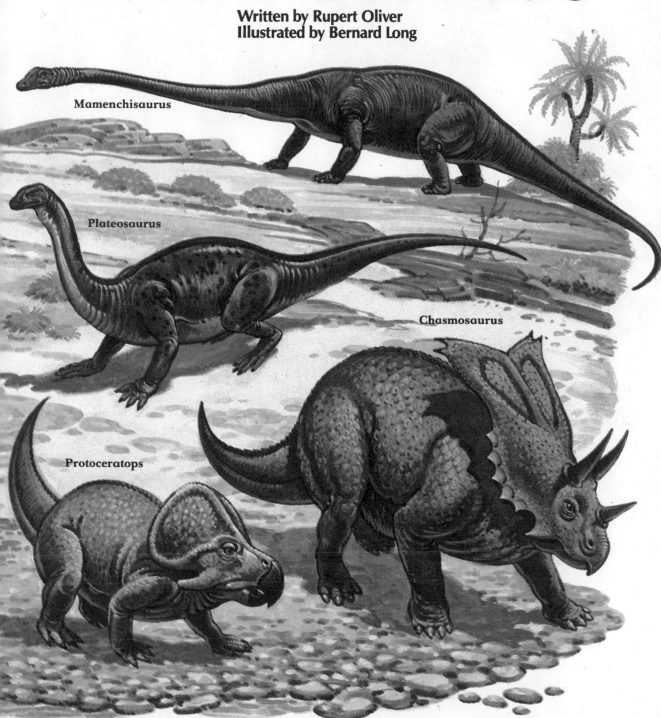

Mamenchisaurus

Plateosaurus

Chasmosaurus

Protoceratops

The twittering of a single bird broke the silence of
the early morning. More and more voices joined
in until the cool air was filled with a resounding
chorus. As the dawn broke in the east the singing
subsided and only the occasional notes drifted
through the trees.

Underneath a particularly large tree a slow
movement disrupted what was otherwise a still scene.
A huge, four-legged dinosaur rose to his feet and
shook his head. Chasmosaurus sniffed the air. It
smelled clean and fresh. It would be another long,
hot day. Chasmosaurus grunted his satisfaction as
the warming rays of the sun broke through and
bathed him in light. Other members of his herd
began to stir for the coming day.

The herd moved out from its resting place beneath the tree. Chasmosaurus was thirsty and the herd drifted toward a stream. A sudden itching by his hind leg worried Chasmosaurus, but he could not reach it to scratch. As he drank, the itching became worse and worse. An insect had planted its egg in Chasmosaurus' hide some days earlier. Now the egg had hatched and the larva was burrowing through Chasmosaurus' skin to reach a vein so that it could suck blood.

Chasmosaurus began to rub his leg against a tree in the hope of relieving the itching. It only got worse. Chasmosaurus kept scratching until the flesh was raw and the larva killed by the pressure. His skin stung, but at least the itching was gone.

As Chasmosaurus was savoring the relief from the infuriating insect a movement caught his eye. Slinking along the far side of the stream was a group of two legged dinosaurs. Chasmosaurus looked at them more carefully. Then he recognized them as Dromaeosaurs. Chasmosaurus was filled with fear and terror. He had seen the way Dromaeosaurs hunted before and it spelled danger for him and his herd.

Chasmosaurus bellowed out a roar signalling
his terror to the herd. Instinctively, the herd drew
closer together and Chasmosaurus hurried to join
them.

The two young Chasmosaurs cowered to the rear while Chasmosaurus and his fellow adults bunched together in a ring. They faced outward and lowered their heads. The Dromaeosaurs advanced toward the Chasmosaurs. The pack of hunters moved cautiously in front of the herd. The solid line of horns and frills which faced the Dromaeosaurs was too much.

After some growling and loud roaring the
Dromaeosaurs lost interest in the Chasmosaurs.
They only stood a chance against armored dinosaurs
if they could catch one on its own. Then, one of the
Dromaeosaurs gave a peculiar growl and all the
pack turned to look toward the stream.

Coming across the stream was a large Parasaurolophus and it had not seen the hungry Dromaeosaurs. Instinctively, the Dromaeosaurs crouched down so that they would not be seen. The Parasaurolophus came closer and closer until suddenly it saw the Dromaeosaurs. It was too late. The Dromaeosaurs could run much faster than the Parasaurolophus. The fierce little hunters soon caught up with their much larger prey. The attacking Dromaeosaurs leaped agilely at the Parasaurolophus, slashing ferociously with their long, sharp claws. It was not long before they had killed the Parasaurolophus and were eating its flesh.

The Chasmosaurs edged slowly away from the dangerous meat eaters. As they moved off, a large Albertosaurus lumbered past them. Albertosaurus had smelled the blood of the Parasaurolophus. Perhaps he could frighten the Dromaeosaurs away and eat his fill of their food.

As soon as the herd was out of sight of the
Dromaeosaurs, it spread out again. Chasmosaurus
moved toward a tasty looking group of bushes. A
sudden thud startled him. Perhaps there was more
danger here. Chasmosaurus began to edge quietly
backward with his head lowered. Then, he heard the
familiar enraged call of a Ceratopsian.

Chasmosaurus pushed around the bushes and found the source of the noise. Two male Styracosaurs were fighting each other. With heads lowered, they were charging at each other and butting with their horns.

A little way off, Chasmosaurus could see a large clump of juicy palms, his favorite food. Chasmosaurus called out in pleasure to the rest of his herd. They followed him over toward the succulent palms.

Already amongst the palms was an Alamosaurus. The long necked Sauropod was feeding on the leaves at the tops of the highest palms. This meant it would not disturb the Chasmosaurs. They ate the leaves and shoots much lower down the plants. As Chasmosaurus sliced off leaf after leaf, he greedily lapped up the delicious juice which flowed from the damaged plant. This was the reason why Chasmosaurus liked palms so much. No other plant gave juice in this way.

Chasmosaurus steadily munched away at the palms. All the time he was moving deeper into the clump of vegetation. After taking hold of a particularly juicy leaf, Chasmosaurus stopped in surprise. Behind the palm had been a Troödon.

The Troödon had just caught a small mammal which it was holding in its jaws. The Troödon was even more surprised than the Chasmosaurus to be disturbed during its meal. Keeping a firm hold on its prey the Troödon scampered off through the foliage. Chasmosaurus carried on eating for a while. Then, he realized that he was some way from the herd. He felt lonely and unprotected so he moved back toward the other Chasmosaurs.

The sun was starting to go down in the West when Chasmosaurus emerged from the palms with the rest of his herd. A Euoplocephalus brushed past Chasmosaurus as it sought a place to bed down for the night. The herd of Chasmosaurs lay down on the edge of the palm clump as the sky turned a deep shade of red. Chasmosaurus was tired and he would need a good night's rest before the next day.

The soft grunts of the sleeping Chasmosaurs whispered through the air as the small mammals crept out to hunt insects and the birds winged home to their nests.

Dimorphodon

Brachiosaurus

Dilophosaurus

Lystrosaurus

Rutiodon

90

Chapter Five

Dimorphodon

Written by Rupert Oliver
Illustrated by Roger Payne

Mamenchisaurus

Plateosaurus

Chasmosaurus

Protoceratops

The roar shattered the dawn stillness of the forest and echoed from tree to tree. The noise of crashing branches and thudding footsteps startled every animal in the forest and set dozens of small animals running for cover. High in the branches of a tree Dimorphodon woke from her sleep with a start. There was something happening, and it might be dangerous.

She twisted to look in the direction of all the noise. Just at that moment the bushes were smashed apart and two large animals tumbled into view. One was a Scelidosaurus, normally a quiet plant-eater, but the other was a Megalosaurus which hunted and ate other dinosaurs. While Scelidosaurus was trying to escape, Megalosaurus was attacking viciously.

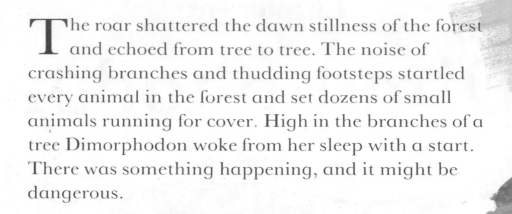

Dimorphodon realized that the struggling dinosaurs were no threat to her, but she kept a wary eye on them just in case. Before long the Megalosaurus clawed the hind leg of Scelidosaurus and brought it down. There was still plenty of fight left in the plant-eater, and its bony back kept the meat-eater at bay for some time. Eventually, Megalosaurus dug his teeth into Scelidosaurus' neck and the plant-eater moved no more.

Megalosaurus had no sooner begun to eat his meal than a pair of Sarcosaurs appeared. They had been attracted by the fight and the smell of blood. Perhaps they would be able to scavenge a meal after Megalosaurus had eaten its fill.

While Megalosaurus gorged itself on the Scelidosaurus, Dimorphodon dropped from her branch and flew away. First she headed for the cliffs along the seashore, where there were usually gusts of wind blowing upwards. If she could find an updraft it would save her a tiring flight.

Dimorphodon soon reached the cliffs beside the sparkling ocean and flew around trying to find an updraft. As soon as she found one, Dimorphodon began to circle tightly. She did not need to flap her wings for the wind was blowing her upwards. As soon as she reached a good height Dimorphodon would turn inland and glide in search of food.

The wind carried Dimorphodon higher and higher into the clear blue sky. Dimorphodon was just getting ready to turn inland when the wind changed. The shift in direction was so sudden that Dimorphodon was caught unawares. The new, strong wind tumbled her over and over in the air. Dimorphodon felt herself falling through the air and it was some time before she could regain her balance.

By the time Dimorphodon had been able to steady herself and begin to fly properly, she was in a strong violent wind. That wind was blowing her out to sea, away from the land. Dimorphodon tried climbing higher, but the wind was just as strong and was still blowing her out to sea. Then she dove down toward the shimmering ocean. At just above wave-top height Dimorphodon pulled out of her dive. Down here the wind was less strong and she could make headway toward the distant shore.

Dimorphodon beat her wings rhythmically as she flew along. Occasionally her wings would dip into the ocean and Dimorphodon nearly lost control. If she plunged into the sea Dimorphodon was not sure if she would be able to get airborne again. Then Dimorphodon became aware of some dark shapes beneath the water. They were moving in the same direction as she was and they were swimming very quickly. Suddenly one of them jumped completely out of the water and then plunged back again with a tremendous splash.

Dimorphodon veered off to one side in alarm. Then another of the creatures jumped from the ocean. This time Dimorphodon got a clear look at it and realized that it was an ichthyosaur and that she had nothing to fear from this creature.

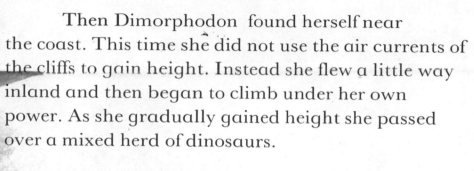

Then Dimorphodon found herself near
the coast. This time she did not use the air currents of
the cliffs to gain height. Instead she flew a little way
inland and then began to climb under her own
power. As she gradually gained height she passed
over a mixed herd of dinosaurs.

The herd were Ohmdenosaurs. These
dinosaurs were plant-eaters which fed off the many
trees and ferns in the area. From Dimorphodon's
vantage point, high in the air, she could see
something that the dinosaurs could not. Just
behind one group of plants was resting a
Metriacanthosaurus. If the plant-eaters got too
close, the Metriacanthosaurus might attack them.

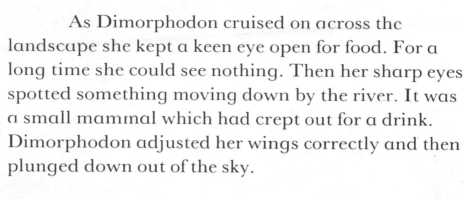

As Dimorphodon cruised on across the landscape she kept a keen eye open for food. For a long time she could see nothing. Then her sharp eyes spotted something moving down by the river. It was a small mammal which had crept out for a drink. Dimorphodon adjusted her wings correctly and then plunged down out of the sky.

Her dive was swift, short and accurate. Within seconds her claws had closed around the mammal and her jaws had snuffed the life out of the little creature. Dimorphodon could eat for the first time that day.

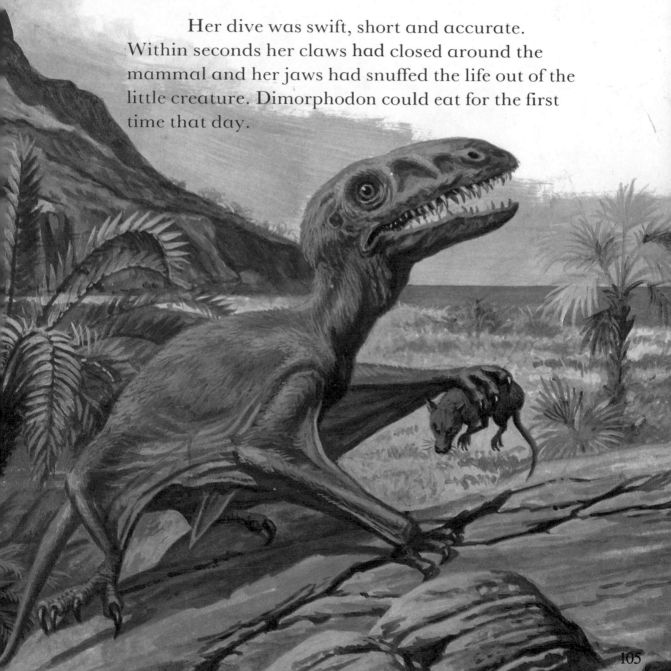

Suddenly, the waters of the river thrashed apart and a long scaly head emerged from the waters. The head was swiftly followed by a powerful body and Dimorphodon recognized it as belonging to a crocodile. Dimorphodon was not very quick at taking off from the ground, but danger was threatening. Desperately, she fluttered her wings and scrambled to take off into the air.

She kept hold of the mammal which she had
killed and was just becoming airborne when the
crocodile arrived. An extra strong flap of her wings
carried Dimorphodon into the air and the jaws of the
crocodile snapped shut just inches beneath her.

With her kill securely grasped in her mouth, Dimorphodon flew back to the upper branches of the forest and roosted. There she ate her fill of the tiny mammal. When she had finished her meal Dimorphodon realized that it was getting late and the shadows were beginning to lengthen. Soon it would be night. Dimorphodon moved to a more comfortable and secure branch on the tree. There she closed her eyes and fell asleep.

Diplodocus

Pteranodon

Woolly Mammoth

Chapter Six
Hypsilophodon

Written by Ron Wilson
Illustrated by Doreen Edwards

Allosaurus

Hypsilophodon

Ichthyosaurus

The young Hypsilophodons had been behind the rock for several hours. In fact since the sun went down. They had slept only for short periods. Several days before they had been driven out by their parents. This was the normal way of things. With their own adult groups there was never enough room for the young as well. Homeless, the young Hypsilophodons had endeavored to find new territory. So far their search had been in vain. Each time they had stopped they had been driven away.

The creatures were very restless. A few slept, but most were awake. One Hypsilophodon stood guard. They took turns sleeping, but this system didn't seem to work well. The Hypsilophodons were waiting for daylight. At least then they could see what was happening. They were also hungry. Perhaps it was the hunger pangs which kept some of the creatures awake.

At the moment there was no noise except for the occasional faint sound as the restless Hypsilophodons moved.

Suddenly there was a whooshing sound. It startled all the Hypsilophodons. They looked at each other, disturbed by the sudden noise. They tried to get closer to the rock for protection. The sound carried around the rock. The young creatures were seized with fear. The sound came from the wind which was sweeping across the rock and tree strewn plain. It increased in force, reaching a high level as it swept around the rock. The Hypsilophodons moved closer together to get away from this new torment.

Almost at the same time as the wind came up, the dawn was beginning to break. A faint light crept over the plains. Now the Hypsilophodons needed to be on their guard. There were some vicious creatures around and they would soon be out looking for their food.

The group of Hypsilophodons had a young male
for a leader. He peered out from behind the rock. In the
distance he could see the large forms of Iguanodons
feeding on the fern-like vegetation.

The urge to feed was great. The Hypsilophodons
had only eaten occasionally. Each time they had
stopped they had been forced to move again because of
the threat from Megalosaurus. In spite of their speed
Hypsilophodons were often caught and eaten by these
ferocious creatures.

The young male Hypsilophodon indicated to the others that it was time to leave. He moved slowly at first, and they followed him. Soon the group was bounding across the plain, easily avoiding the boulders.

The leader stopped by a shrub laden with ripe berries. Soon all the Hypsilophodons were feeding eagerly. For the first time in days they were able to eat without disturbance.

Suddenly the ground started to shudder. The group stopped feeding. Panic struck. They fled in all directions. They sought refuge behind anything they could find. Their panic was unnecessary. The disturbance had been caused by the approach of several Polacanthus. Like Iguanodons and Hypsilophodons, Polacanthus were also plant-eaters. They too had spotted the luscious berries.

The Hypsilophodons stayed hidden for some time. The leader, realizing that it was a false alarm, looked out from behind the tree trunk where he had taken cover. He called gently, a call which told the others that all was well.

They came out from their hiding places and assembled around the leader. He waited, realizing that not all the group had returned. In the distance he could see the form of a Hypsilophodon making its way slowly toward the group.

The leader left the others and made his way quickly to the distant creature. It soon became obvious what the problem was. In making for safety a young female Hypsilophodon had damaged a leg. She was limping badly. The male stayed with her as she made her way to the rest of the group. They eventually rejoined the others.

The young male leader led the female to a rock. By a series of vocal sounds, a young male was assigned to look after the injured female. Another male was to gather food and take it back to the two Hypsilophodons sheltering behind the rock.

The rest of the group made their way to shrubs laden with berries. This time they were more cautious. Members took turns guarding and warning the others if danger threatened.

Several large Pteranodons flew low over the plain. They were no threat to the Hypsilophodons. However, the creatures did not know this. They scattered, making for the nearest shelters. After the Pteranodons had gone they came out and regrouped to continue their feeding.

Suddenly the still air was shattered by the sound of terrible cries. The Hypsilophodons stopped feeding. They looked across the plain, not sure of where the noise was coming from. Some distance away were three Iguanodons. Two were engaged in battle. Two males were fighting over the same female.

The young Hypsilophodons were anxious to see what was happening. They moved closer to the scene of the action. The Iguanodons relied on their strength when fighting.

When the first Hypsilophodons arrived at the site of the conflict the two Iguanodons were going around in circles. Neither seemed to be winning the contest.

Suddenly there was a piercing shriek and the action was over. One Iguanodon plunged to its death over a cliff. The victor looked over the edge. Then he turned to the female and they continued to feed as if nothing had happened.

With nothing more to see the Hypsilophodons returned to their feeding activities. They had found a bush filled with berries some 150 feet from the two resting Hypsilophodons. At first they were ever on the lookout for danger. Gradually they all became so engrossed in satisfying their hunger that they forgot about their enemies.

A short, sharp cry of terror made the Hypsilophodons look up from their meal. The sound came from the rocks. They saw the reason for the anguished cry. A pair of Megalosaurus had crept up on the two Hypsilophodons. Now the young dinosaurs stood little chance. Soon they were in the grip of these powerful flesh-eaters. Faint cries of terror reached the other Hypsilophodons. They were rooted to the spot. The leader realized that there was little they could do to save two of their kind. At a signal from him the rest of the group made off as fast as their long, powerful legs would carry them.

The two unfortunate Hypsilophodons struggled. However, their efforts were in vain. They were no match for the much larger and more powerful Megalosaurus. It didn't take long for the creatures to eat their fill.

Meanwhile the fleeing Hypsilophodons had found shelter behind a large rocky outcrop. This was far enough from the scene of the attack. They rested here. Soon they would have to go off again to seek yet more food and face the ever-present danger from their flesh-eating enemies.

Diplodocus

Pteranodon

Woolly Mammoth

Chapter Seven

Ichthyosaurus

Written by Ron Wilson
Illustrated by Doreen Edwards

Allosaurus

Hypsilophodon

Ichthyosaurus

The young Ichthyosaurus was the smallest and weakest of the family. She had not received as much food as her brothers and sisters when she was an infant. She was still a weakling when the others were ready to leave their mother. As with all Ichthyosaurs, the young stayed with the female for several months. One by one, the others had gone their separate ways; only she remained. Only then, did she get all the attention and food that she needed.

Today something was not quite right. The mother Ichthyosaurus had become very restless. Her young offspring wasn't sure what the signs meant. She had never seen her mother like this before. The mother was driving the young one away from her.

Not realizing what her mother meant, she had returned repeatedly. Each time the mother became more agitated and drove the young one off.

The young Ichthyosaurus was confused. She wondered what the problem was. She stayed away. However, since she had never been left alone before, she kept her mother in sight.

As the young Ichthyosaurus swam around she noticed a large rocky outcrop. She moved toward it. As she did so she made many backward glances to ensure that her mother didn't disappear completely.

Unlike her brothers and sisters the young female had never engaged in the wild diving and swimming activities that they had. She had never had enough energy. Now somehow she managed to find enough strength to power her flipper-like paddles so that she could maneuver her way toward the jagged rock. The rock would provide suitable hiding places, and from its safety she could watch her mother's movements.

The rock was extremely large. She came closer to it. Crags hung out from it making the water around it very dark. Fear overcame her. She had never been on her own before. She made for a small overhanging ledge, disturbing a shoal of Pholidophorus. She sidled gently toward the ledge looking very carefully for other signs of life. It wasn't easy to see in the dim light.

The juvenile Ichthyosaurus suddenly felt something crash into her. A larger Ichthyosaurus had been using the same place for shelter. As the female moved back she crashed into another ledge.

Panicking, she left the safety of the rock. In the confusion she had lost sight of her mother. She didn't know what to do or where to go.

Then she spotted the dull outline of an adult Ichthyosaurus in the distance. She wasn't sure whether it was her mother. Slowly she moved toward the outline. It became clearer. She recognized the familiar figure. By now the young female was so relieved that she had forgotten her mother's earlier reactions. As she approached her mother, she was driven off again. This time, her mother was angrier than before. She lashed out with her large flipper-like paddles, missing the young creature by inches.

The young Ichthyosaurus was more than puzzled by this latest outburst. She circled around for a few minutes. She wasn't certain what to do now. She had never left her mother before — not even to catch her own food.

She continued to swim around cautiously. Each time another creature came by she backed away. Most were smaller than she was, but she had not really been taught how to fend for herself.

Short of air the young female made her way
slowly to the surface to fill her lungs. She had never
done this before on her own. Now instinct told her she
must do it. She moved upward.

One thing she had learned from her mother was
that danger often lurked above the water. It took her a
few minutes to reach the top. She paused just under the
surface for a few minutes. She looked upward.

Cautiously she poked her long snout out of the
water. She looked around. She was very close to the
shore. Looking up she could see the outlines of
Pterosaurs. As she watched, several of them left their
perches on the cliffs above her and dived toward the
sea.

Fear overcame the young Ichthyosaurus. For a few seconds she remained motionless, her head poking above the water.

Then she realized that the Pterodactyls were coming toward her. They had spotted a shoal of fish. She did not realize this; she thought they were coming for her.

She quickly gulped as much air as she could and withdrew below the surface. As she looked up she could see the form of the Pterodactyls flying toward the water.

The Ichthyosaurus dived quickly to a lower
level. On her way down she passed her mother coming
up. She slowed down as the two approached. Her
mother ignored her and continued toward the surface.
The young Ichthyosaurus turned for a moment so that
she could follow her mother's upward movement. She
paused, started to follow, and then decided against it.
Instead she circled slowly waiting for her mother's
return. She did not have to wait long. The large form
of an Ichthyosaurus appeared. Keeping her distance the
young creature followed in the older creature's wake.

The jagged rock appeared in the distance. The
older female made for it. The young one followed.
There was plenty of room for both of them to shelter.

As she neared the rock the young Ichthyosaurus could see clouds of mud rising. She paused for a moment, unsure of what was happening. Suddenly the form of a much larger Ichthyosaurus came toward her at great speed. It was very angry and left behind a trail of blood. She dived to one side and followed its movements. As she gazed at the fleeing creature it turned around and came back toward her. The trail of blood grew wider. Again she moved away.

The angry, injured Ichthyosaurus continued on its way toward the rock. More mud flew up. The young creature was curious. Carefully, she made her way to the rock. Two male Ichthyosaurs were locked in combat. A young female watched them. Eventually, the wounded male was driven off. The victorious creature turned to the waiting female.

The cloudy water was beginning to settle and the unattached female peered into the distance. She could now make out the outline of the rock.

She swam slowly around it, carefully looking into every nook and cranny. She had never really surveyed it before. It was massive and there were numerous hiding places.

The young Ichthyosaurus's survey took her a long while. She was very careful. She came to one overhanging ledge. She caught sight of a large tail fin. She hid behind an outcrop and studied it. She could see the rest of the creature. She recognized the form — it was her mother.

Her first instinct was to go toward her. She didn't. She looked on rather bewildered at her mother's actions. Then she caught sight of what she thought was the form of a small Ichthyosaurus. Her mother had given birth to her next offspring.

Now the juvenile Ichthyosaurus knew that she
was on her own. She turned around quickly, as
something prodded her gently. There, swimming close
by, was another young Ichthyosaurus. The newcomer
swam away and then came back toward her. She
realized it was a young male.

The moment had really come for her to break her ties with her mother. It was now time to mate and start her own family. She moved off, turning frequently to glance at the young Ichthyosaurus watched over by the older female.

Rhamphorhynchus

Pteranodon

Pterodactyl

Ankylosaurus

Dimetrodon

Iguanodon

Tricondon

150

Chapter Eight

Iguanodon

Written by Rupert Oliver
Illustrated by Bernard Long

Archaeopteryx

Ichthyosaurus

Plesiosaurus

Deinonychus

Nothosaurus

Iguanodon stared into the sky and sniffed the air. He could smell rain, but it was not raining here. Far away in the mountains there was a storm. Rain was falling heavily there. That was what Iguanodon could smell.

The herd to which Iguanodon belonged had left the great forest and was moving out on to the plains. On the plains grew many delicious plants for the herd to eat. Iguanodon moved off down the slope to join his herd. He did not want to be left on his own. In the herd he would be safer from attack by a fierce Megalosaurus. This dreaded meat-eater was always ready to make a meal out of an Iguanodon.

As the herd moved out on to the flat plains they kept a careful watch in case of danger. All they could see was a group of huge Cetiosauriscus. These large dinosaurs were feeding on a clump of trees in the distance.

Iguanodon went down on all fours to eat some leaves from a cycad plant. He reached out with his tongue and took a firm hold on some foliage. Iguanodon used his horny beak to nip off the leaves. Then he chewed the food with his flat teeth.

As Iguanodon pushed further into the clump of cycads there was a strange rustling sound. Suddenly three small two-legged dinosaurs emerged. They were Hypsilophodons. The Hypsilophodons looked at Iguanodon and then ran off toward the forest. They ran very quickly, bounding from one leg to the other. Iguanodon watched them for a while. Then he continued eating the juicy cycads. High above him Pterosaurs flapped and swooped through the air.

153

The large, rolling plain stretched as far as
Iguanodon could see. It was like a vast green carpet
of cycads, horsetails and rushes. Iguanodon
looked hungrily at a group of maidenhair trees and
monkey-puzzle trees a short distance off. They would
be much tastier than the redwoods in the forest.
The herd moved toward the clump of trees.

When Iguanodon looked back toward the mountains, he could see that it was still raining. However, the plains were quite dry. The rivers were almost empty. The Goniopholis had to stay in small pools of water to keep cool in the mid-day sun. The Goniopholis took no notice of the Iguanodon herd as they crossed the dry river bed.

After stopping to browse on a particularly tempting patch of horsetails, the herd reached the clump of trees. Iguanodon stretched up into the trees to reach the leaves. Using his tongue to grasp the leaves, Iguanodon munched away.

For several hours the herd stayed in the trees, then some of the Iguanodons wandered away to eat the cycads, ferns and horsetails. Others stayed at the edge of the trees and ate the leaves. Iguanodon moved deeper into the trees. He was looking for the juicy magnolia shrub which often grew under the trees. Then, Iguanodon saw some strange shapes moving in the shadows of the trees. He looked closer and suddenly gave a cry of fright and alarm.

Hiding in the trees were four Megalosaurs. These ferocious dinosaurs had powerful claws and teeth and they were hungry. Iguanodon smashed his way through the undergrowth, bellowing a warning to the rest of the herd. Behind him he could hear the thumping of the heavy feet of the Megalosaurs. As Iguanodon burst from the trees the rest of his herd scattered in alarm. Iguanodon ran on in a panic. The fierce hunters were gaining on him. He knew what would happen to him if they caught him. His life was at stake.

Iguanodon was running as fast as he could, but the Megalosaurs were overtaking him. Iguanodon's powerful legs carried him to the banks of the dried-up river. He slid down the bank to the river bed. The hungry meat-eaters followed Iguanodon even here. As Iguanodon and the Megalosaurs raced along the dry river bed the Goniopholis scattered in alarm. Iguanodon looked behind him. The Megalosaurs had almost caught him. Then, he heard a strange and terrible rumbling sound.

Looking ahead of him Iguanodon could see
a wall of water rushing toward him. The heavy rain in the
mountains had filled the mountain streams with
millions of gallons of water. That water had formed a
flash flood that was pouring down the dry river bed.

When the Megalosaurs saw the rush of
water they tried to run away. They were too late.
The terrific force of the rushing water hit Iguanodon
seconds later. It swept him off his feet and tumbled
him over and over. Then, it smashed into the Megalosaurs
and swept them along as well.

Iguanodon felt himself being thrown around by
the water. He was being spun around by the force of
the flood. Finally Iguanodon's head rose above the
surface. Iguanodon took a gulp of air. He looked
around and saw the Megalosaurs were also being
thrown about by the water. The rushing torrent
pulled Iguanodon back under the surface.

Iguanodon was dizzy with all the tumbling. The force of the water frightened him almost as much as the Megalosaurs had done. There was nothing he could do to avoid being swept along.

After a long time Iguanodon felt firm ground beneath his feet. He managed to pull himself free of the rushing waters. Iguanodon was very tired and badly bruised. He fell on the bank to rest.

When he felt stronger Iguanodon looked around. The river bed was now full of water. The Megalosaurs were nowhere to be seen. The flash flood must have carried them much further downstream. Perhaps they had been drowned.

Nearby, Iguanodon could see a Polacanthus browsing on some ferns. The Polacanthus turned to look at Iguanodon. Then he went back to his meal. In the distance Iguanodon saw a herd of Iguanodons. He decided to join them.

Wearily, Iguanodon stood up on his aching legs. He set off across the plain. He passed the Polacanthus but soon had to stop to rest. Iguanodon was very tired after his adventures. After a while he went on toward the other Iguanodons.

When he was close to them he realized that they
were members of his own herd. Iguanodon joined the
herd. He was glad to be back with his own kind.
Iguanodon fed on a clump of cycads. Soon it would
be evening and the herd would settle down for the night.

Dimorphodon

Brachiosaurus

Dilophosaurus

Lystrosaurus

Rutiodon

Chapter Nine

Mamenchisaurus

Written by Rupert Oliver
Illustrated by Andrew Howatt

Mamenchisaurus

Plateosaurus

Chasmosaurus

Protoceratops

It had been raining even before the sun had risen.
It was almost noon and the rain was still falling.
Mamenchisaurus bit off a tasty mouthful of leaves
from the high branches of the tree. He chewed them
quickly and then swallowed them, taking another
mouthful as he did so. Mamenchisaurus was always
hungry and spent most of his time eating.

Around the small clump of trees at which Mamenchisaurus was feeding stood the rest of his herd. Mamenchisaurus looked around to make sure they were still there. He always felt safer when he was near his herd. The rain was not falling quite so heavily now and a ray of sunshine burst through the clouds.

Mamenchisaurus caught sight of some tasty leaves near the top of a tree further into the woods. He moved forward to get near enough to eat them. As Mamenchisaurus pushed through the dense undergrowth, he realized that he was on the edge of a river bank. Mamenchisaurus moved forward and then he felt the ground fall slightly. He looked around in alarm as the river bank gave way beneath his great weight.

He slithered down a steep, muddy
slope until he reached the bottom.

Mamenchisaurus roared out a distress signal
and the herd appeared at the top of the slope.
Mamenchisaurus tried to climb up the slope, but the
mud was too slippery.

The other Mamenchisaurs found they could not help him, so, after a while, they moved back to the trees to continue eating. Mamenchisaurus felt very alone. He had never been away from the herd before and he felt vulnerable. He had to get back to his herd. He tried climbing the slope again, but just slithered back down. Perhaps there would be a way out further along the river.

Mamenchisaurus splashed along the river, his feet sinking into the ooze with each step. Suddenly a small Gongubusaurus dashed from among a small clump of horsetails and scampered up the river bank. Mamenchisaurus could also climb the bank here, for the slope did not seem to be as steep.

Treading very carefully, Mamenchisaurus managed to heave his great bulk up the steep slope without sliding backward. Mamenchisaurus looked around for his herd, but it was nowhere in sight. Mamenchisaurus began to plod off in the direction from which he had come. Perhaps he would find his herd that way.

Mamenchisaurus had not gone very far when two huge shapes emerged from some trees in front of him. At once he recognized the large creatures as Yangchuanosaurs. Mamenchisaurus was very frightened because Yangchuanosaurs were ferocious hunters which were always ready to make a meal of plant-eaters such as Mamenchisaurus.

Mamenchisaurus turned to move away, but
the Yangchuanosaurs had already seen him. The
hunters were hungry and could run faster than
Mamenchisaurus could walk. Soon they began to
overtake him. Mamenchisaurus knew that he could
not escape. He only had one chance.

He stood still with his back toward the
advancing hunters and waited. The fierce-looking
Yangchuanosaurs came running forward, with their
fearsome jaws and claws, eager for an easy meal.

When they were almost upon Mamenchisaurus, he lashed out with his tail. The swinging tail caught one of the Yangchuanosaurs just below its arm and lifted it right off its feet. The force of the blow knocked the dinosaur sideways and sent it sprawling heavily on the ground. The second hunter stopped in amazement and quickly backed out of range of Mamenchisaurus' tail.

The Yangchuanosaurus which the frightened Mamenchisaurus had hit lay on the ground moaning in pain. The other hunter came forward to help its companion but did not attempt any attack on Mamenchisaurus. Mamenchisaurus moved off, but kept a careful eye on the Yangchuanosaurs because they might still try to attack again.

Mamenchisaurus was worried. He wanted to rejoin his herd, but the Yangchuanosaurs were between him and the herd. Then, he saw a group of sauropods in the distance. Perhaps his herd had moved. Mamenchisaurus moved toward the sauropods, passing a Tuojiangosaurus on his way.

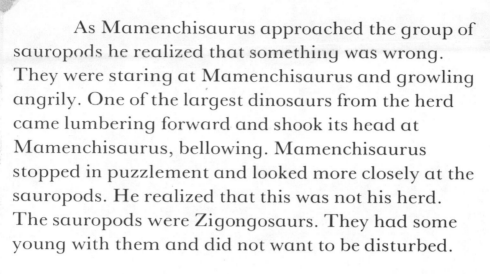

As Mamenchisaurus approached the group of
sauropods he realized that something was wrong.
They were staring at Mamenchisaurus and growling
angrily. One of the largest dinosaurs from the herd
came lumbering forward and shook its head at
Mamenchisaurus, bellowing. Mamenchisaurus
stopped in puzzlement and looked more closely at the
sauropods. He realized that this was not his herd.
The sauropods were Zigongosaurs. They had some
young with them and did not want to be disturbed.

Mamenchisaurus did not want any trouble so
he moved away from the Zigongosaurs, taking care
not to stray toward the Yangchuanosaurus.

Mamenchisaurus lumbered on across the countryside until he came to the top of a low rise. From the hill he could see out across the landscape and he looked for his herd. Mamenchisaurus was suddenly startled when something leaped from the undergrowth. It was only a Sinocoelurus chasing a small mammal. Fortunately, it was no danger to Mamenchisaurus. As Mamenchisaurus gazed out from his hill he saw a group of sauropods emerge from some trees. The sauropods looked like other Mamenchisaurs. Perhaps this was his herd.

Mamenchisaurus moved down the slope in the direction of the herd.

Mamenchisaurus plodded slowly across the ground and roared out a signal of recognition. This was his herd. The members of the herd turned around when they heard Mamenchisaurus roar. As they realized that this was their missing member they, too, roared in recognition.

It was getting near to evening now, and the rain clouds were beginning to build up again. The herd looked for somewhere to rest for the night. There was a small clump of trees nearby and they moved toward it. Mamenchisaurus had not eaten for some time and was very hungry indeed. While the rest of the herd settled down to sleep, Mamenchisaurus continued to eat in order to satisfy his hunger. It was dark and the moon was high in the sky before Mamenchisaurus settled down to sleep.

Brontosaurus
(Apatosaurus)

Pteranodon

Cetiosaurus

Dimetrodon

Iguanodon

Stegosaurus

190

Chapter Ten

Triceratops

Written by Angela Sheehan
Illustrated by John Francis

Tyrannosaurus

Triceratops

Parasaurolophus

Ornithomimus

Ankylosaurus

A hairy animal, no bigger than a mouse, watched Triceratops as she kicked a blanket of sand over the three eggs she had just laid. The sand would keep them warm and well hidden while the young reptiles inside the shells grew big enough to hatch.

Laying her eggs and making them safe had been hard work for Triceratops. Now she was tired; too tired even to notice the little mammal or the other dinosaur that had sneaked up to watch her. The dinosaur, Ornithomimus, kept his thin body close behind a tree while Triceratops struggled clumsily over the rocks, looking for a place to rest before the sun grew too hot.

As soon as Triceratops had lumbered away, the
little mammal scurried from its hiding place to nose for
worms and beetles among the ferns. He was hungry.
So too was Ornithomimus. And Ornithomimus liked
nothing better than to eat the eggs of other dinosaurs.

Slyly, Ornithomimus picked his way to the nest and bent his long neck to brush the sand from his prize. The first shell broke with a crack, and the yolk spilled out. Ornithomimus licked up the sweet, warm liquid.

The egg tasted delicious. But it was the only one that Ornithomimus ate. For a frightful roar sounded behind him. No need to look, he took to his legs, leaping swiftly and nimbly over the rocks. Close behind him came the harsh sound of clawed feet, crashing and crunching over the ground. The monstrous Tyrannosaurus was bearing down on him. Only speed or slyness could save Ornithomimus now.

Triceratops knew nothing of the robbing of her nest, nor of the chase that followed. She rested in a thicket of giant ferns as the sun rose high in the sky. Shaded by the broad green fronds, she drifted into a deep sleep. Some hours later, she was woken by the thud of heavy raindrops and the rumble of thunder. The rain beat down, drenching and flattening the ferns.

After the storm, the sun came out to dry the plants. Steam rose from the fronds and the smell of their freshness filled the air. Triceratops ate her first meal of the day. Slicing the greenery with her beak-like jaws, she munched her way through the thicket. Birds sang in the trees above her, small mammals scampered by her feet, and pterosaurs clung to the tree trunks.

Suddenly, there was silence. The birds ceased
to sing, the mammals crept into their holes, the
pterosaurs took to the air. Triceratops stood stock
still. The only noise that could be heard was the
sound of branches snapping beneath the heavy tread of
Tyrannosaurus. All the animals waited in terror.

One dinosaur, Ankylosaurus, was standing directly in the brute's path. He sank to the ground and drew his legs in under his armor. Tyrannosaurus circled around and around him, roaring in fury. But Ankylosaurus was like a rock, too solid for tooth or claw to pierce, and too heavy to move. There was no way through his armor.

Tyrannosaurus had only one hope: to turn him over and attack his soft belly. Triceratops and the other animals watched from a safe distance as the great creature tried to heave him over. But no matter how hard he tried, Tyrannosaurus could not shift the stubborn stone.

Suddenly Tyrannosaurus gave up, and, in an instant, turned his anger on Triceratops. But instead of fleeing, she stood her ground, head down, as the great animal charged. Unable to stop in time, the savage creature screamed in pain as Triceratops thrust one of her great horns into his thigh. Now the mighty dinosaur could only limp away. The blood from his wound left a red trail in the ferns.

The other creatures in the wood were safe now. Tyrannosaurus would not bother them again until his wound had healed. Slowly the mammals crept from hiding and the birds began to sing and flutter in the trees. Triceratops plodded to the lake where she could drink and bathe. And, after some time, Ankylosaurus, too, was brave enough to push out his head and move carefully away. He looked about him as he went and swung his heavy tail from side to side.

The lake water was warm and silky. Triceratops wallowed in the shallows and bit the tasty tops of the horsetails that grew there. As the shadows began to lengthen, the insects stopped their buzzing in the magnolia flowers. And a chill wind began to blow. Triceratops clambered up the slippery bank, her feet squelching in the soft mud. She would soon have to find a place to sleep.

As she left the lake, Triceratops heard the distant croaks of pterosaurs as they sought their nightly perches on the cliffs. She also heard a strange cracking noise that made her stop in her tracks. Peering through the twilight, she saw two Stegoceras dinosaurs charging towards each other. With a tremendous crash, their thick skulls clashed. Again and again they charged, while the rest of the herd looked on in silence.

Soon the battle was over. The weaker
Stegoceras reeled backwards, unhurt, but unable to
stand another attack. The other strode away, with his
head held high and the rest of the herd following. As
Triceratops went on her way, she passed the weaker
one, trailing far behind his herd.

Now it was almost night and the wind blew colder. With no fur or feathers to keep her warm, Triceratops had to find a warm place to sleep. She headed for her favorite spot. It was a rocky hollow near where she had laid her eggs that morning. The rocks shielded her from the wind and a pile of dry ferns kept her warm and out of sight of any enemies. She could sleep safe and sound——until tomorrow.

Facts about Dinosaurs
Interesting facts about . . .
Allosaurus

Head
huge with
bony crest.
Massive jaws
with extremely
powerful teeth
for tearing
flesh

Neck
rather short,
very strong
and powerful

Arms
short with
three fingers
and strong,
sharp claws

Body
half as long as
tail and heavy

Legs
heavy with
three toes on
each foot

Length 36 feet (maximum 42 fe
Height 16 feet
Weight between 1 and 2 tons

Tail
long and he
out to help
balance bo

A skeleton of Allosaurus compared to a human form to show differences in size

Allosaurus belonged to a group of dinosaurs called Carnosaurs. The word carnosaur means "flesh-
lizard". This tells us that Allosaurus and its
relatives fed on meat. It probably did this by killing other animals.

The carnosaurs are divided into many families.
Allosaurus belonged to a family called the
Allosaurids. They were such vicious creatures that
they have earned the title "tigers of the Jurassic
age". More than half of the creature's length was
made up of its tail. The head was huge and there
was a thick neck which the creature could move
easily.

The name Allosaurus means "different lizard".
This dinosaur had other names including
Labrosaurus and Antrodemus.

What size was Allosaurus?

Like all the carnosaurs Allosaurus was an extremely large dinosaur. The average length of one of
these creatures was about 36 feet. However, there
have been reports of Allosaurus which have
measured as much as 42 feet in length. The largest
of all the Allosaurus discovered was reckoned to
have been 16 feet tall.

Several Allosaurus remains have been found.

Scientists have worked out that they would have
weighed between 1 and 2 tons.

When did Allosaurus live?

Allosaurus lived in Jurassic times (193-136 million
years ago). So far remains of Allosaurus have
been found in several parts of the world. These include Australia, Africa and North America. Scientists think that these creatures also lived in Asia as
well.

What was Allosaurus like?

Allosaurus was a large dinosaur. The head was
very big, and strangely shaped. It had a crest
along the nose. As well as this crest, there were
also some lumps on the head. No one has yet been
able to say why they were there.

How did Allosaurus walk?

Scientists who looked at the remains of Allosaurus
were able to tell how it moved. Although the front
legs had large talons, useful for holding animals
which it caught for food, these legs were not
suitable for walking on. Allosaurus walked
upright on its hind legs.

What did Allosaurus eat?

Allosaurus was a meat-eating dinosaur. It had to hunt and kill large plant-eating creatures like Diplodocus. To be able to do this, Allosaurus had extremely large teeth and a very big jaw. To help it grip its prey, Allosaurus had three fingers on each of the front legs. At the end of each of the fingers were long, sharp talons.

Although the creatures which Allosaurus attacked for food probably weighed five or more times as much as Allosaurus, its sharp blade-like teeth and talons would help it kill its food. Allosaurus probably hunted in packs.

Scientists are sure that Allosaurus went out hunting for these large creatures. In one case its fossil footprints have been found in the mud of a lagoon. As well as the footprints which Allosaurus left, there were also footprints of the plant-eaters which it was following. Once Allosaurus had caught its food, it could use its sharp dagger-like teeth to tear out the insides. The teeth were then used to tear off large pieces of meat. The jaw of Allosaurus was so large that it could swallow huge chunks of flesh. Not everyone agrees about the food which Allosaurus ate. As we have seen some people thought that the dinosaur stalked and killed its food. However, there are others who think that Allosaurus and its relatives were too large and clumsy for this. They think that these large creatures had to scavange from dead animals.

A small brain

Although dinosaurs like Allosaurus had very large heads, their brains were very small. The skulls were large because they carried massive teeth. The bones which made up the skull were very thin. However there were areas over the eyes which were made of thicker bone. This helped to protect the eyes.

All three creatures were flesh-eating dinosaurs. Ceratosaurus was unusual because it had a small horn on its nose. Tyrannosaurus was about 39 feet long; Allosaurus was around 36 feet in length and Ceratosaurus was smaller — between 15 and 20 feet

Tyrannosaurus

Allosaurus

Ceratosaurus

Archaeopteryx and Jurassic Europe

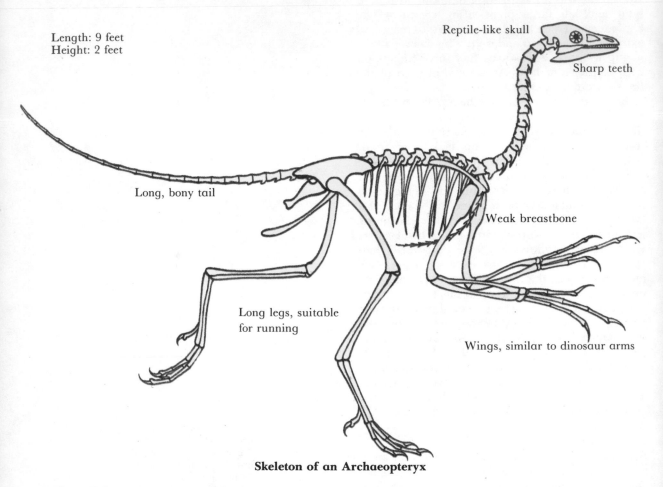

Length: 9 feet
Height: 2 feet

Reptile-like skull

Sharp teeth

Long, bony tail

Weak breastbone

Long legs, suitable for running

Wings, similar to dinosaur arms

Skeleton of an Archaeopteryx

When did Archaeopteryx live?

Archaeopteryx lived during the Age of the Dinosaurs. Scientists have divided this Age into three periods, First the Triassic which began about 225 million years ago and lasted for 35 million years. Next the Jurassic which lasted from 190 million years ago until 136 million years ago. The last period of the Age of Dinosaurs is called the Cretaceous period and lasted until about 64 million years ago. Fossils of Archaeopteryx have been found in rocks that date from about halfway through the Jurassic.

Where did Archaeopteryx live?

All the fossils of Archaeopteryx have been found in a rather small area of Germany. We therefore deduce that it lived in central Europe during the Jurassic. However, the bones of Archaeopteryx are very small and fragile. It is possible that this early bird lived in other parts of the world, but that it was only fossilised in Germany. A mid-Jurassic fossil has been found in North America which may belong to a relative of Archaeopteryx. Unfortunately nobody is sure that it was a bird.

The life of Archaeopteryx

Ever since the first fossil of Archaeopteryx was found in 1861, scientists have been trying to decide how it lived. There have been many suggestions and even today scientists do not all agree with each other. There are two main theories about the life style of this early bird.

The first theory sees Archaeopteryx as a tree-living animal. Archaeopteryx had curved, sharp claws on its front and hind limbs. Such claws would be useful for clinging to tree trunks and branches. Furthermore the big toe grew in such a way that it could be used for holding onto branches. The wing muscles of Archaeopteryx were surprisingly weak. There was no way that it could take off from the ground. The best Archaeopteryx could manage would have been a short glide from a tree branch. The picture that emerges from this evidence is of a tree-climber that could glide to escape danger or catch prey.

However, some scientists point out that the legs of Archaeopteryx are built for fast running on the ground. They also point out that the broad wings could have been used as insect traps or for display purposes. These scientists picture Archaeopteryx as living on the ground, eating insects and scavenging. They also suppose that feathers did not evolve to aid flight. They think that they developed as insulation to keep Archaeopteryx warm and only later were used for flight. In this book we have shown Archaeopteryx in both these roles.

The ancestors of Archaeopteryx

Archaeopteryx was a remarkable animal. It was the earliest bird that we know of, yet in many ways it was more like a reptile than a bird. It had teeth, a bony tail and a rather small breastbone, with no deep keel of bone for the attachment of flying muscles. It has often been said that Archaeopteryx is really a reptile that is halfway through evolving into a bird. The fossils of Archaeopteryx prove that birds evolved from reptiles millions of years ago. Unfortunately scientists cannot agree as to which type of reptile evolved into birds.

Some scientists point out that the creatures that became crocodiles could have become birds, others think that we have not yet found any fossils of the reptiles that became birds. A recent theory states that birds evolved from a type of dinosaur. There was a group of small, running dinosaurs called coelurosaurs whose skeletons were very like that of Archaeopteryx. Compsognathus and Teinurosaurus were both coelurosaurs. The new theory states that Archaeopteryx evolved from dinosaurs like Compsognathus. Nobody has yet been able to prove any of these theories and the ancestors of Archaeopteryx remain unknown.

The world of Archaeopteryx

Europe in mid-Jurassic times was very different from modern Europe. The forests were made up of cycads, conifers, giant ferns and strange plants called Williamsonias. There were no true flowering plants. The animals were just as unfamiliar. The only mammals to be seen were tiny shrew-like creatures which probably only ventured forth at night.

Several species of Pelorosaurus are known to have existed, but from the fragmentary remains found so far, an accurate size of this dinosaur is not known. It was probably about 50 feet long. It lived on vegetation and was hunted by such fearsome dinosaurs as Megalosaurus. This 20 foot long meat-eater was a powerful killer. Dryosaurus was about 10 feet long. It was one of the earliest of the Ornithopods, a group of dinosaurs that later became important. There were several species of Elaphrosaurus, one up to 20 feet long. Elaphrosaurus was an ostrich dinosaur, related to the coelurosaurs. Some of the animals of the Jurassic would be familiar, among them the lizard and butterfly caught by Archaeopteryx. While Archaeopteryx was a poor flier, there was one group of animals that had conquered the air, the pterosaurs. Rhamphorhynchus, a type of pterosaur, can be seen on page 30.

Some present-day descendants of Archaeopteryx

Owl

Eagle

Sparrow

Bird of Paradise

Brontosaurus and the Jurassic World

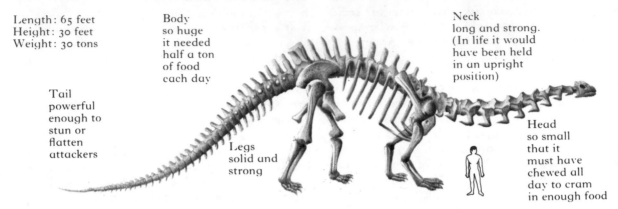

Length: 65 feet
Height: 30 feet
Weight: 30 tons

Body
so huge
it needed
half a ton
of food
each day

Neck
long and strong.
(In life it would
have been held
in an upright
position)

Tail
powerful
enough to
stun or
flatten
attackers

Legs
solid and
strong

Head
so small
that it
must have
chewed all
day to cram
in enough food

The skeleton of Brontosaurus compared in size with a man

"Thunder Lizard"

The name Brontosaurus means "thunder lizard". Imagine the noise a herd of them would have made as they trundled along, and you will realize what a good name it is. Brontosaurus is also now called Apatosaurus.

Brontosaurus was one of the largest animals ever to live. It belonged to a group of plant-eating dinosaurs, called sauropods. There were lots of different kinds, but they were all huge (see opposite page). Diplodocus was longer than Brontosaurus; Brachiosaurus was bigger and heavier. He must have weighed as much as 100 tons. Unlike the other sauropods, his front legs were larger than the back ones.

When did Brontosaurus live?

Brontosaurus lived 150 million years ago during the Jurassic period. This was the middle period of the Age of Dinosaurs. The earlier period is called the Triassic and the one following it the Cretaceous.

Plants of the Jurassic

During the Jurassic, the climate was warm, and the earth was covered with dense growths of ferns and other plants for the dinosaurs to eat. Palm-like cycads with thick trunks and huge leaves grew everywhere. There were conifer trees, such as pines and redwoods, and there were lots of maidenhair, or ginkgo, trees. They were the chief food for the brontosaurs—you can see their fan-shaped leaves on page 57.

Animals of the Jurassic

Many fierce flesh-eating dinosaurs lived at the same time as Brontosaurus. The largest was Allosaurus (see page 11), a ferocious monster that strode about on its huge back legs. The adult sauropods were probably safe from the meat-eaters. Like elephants today, they were just too big to be attacked. But the younger brontosaurs and old, weak ones were probably easy prey. A smaller plant-eater, such as Stegosaurus (see pages 54 & 64) would also have given Allosaurus little trouble.

Small meat-eaters would never have tackled the armored plant-eaters or the sauropods. They probably fed on dead animals (as Ornitholestes is doing on page 55), or on the remains of the kills of the larger dinosaurs. They may also have trailed the herds of plant-eaters to pick up small lizards and insects disturbed by the dinosaurs' feet.

Land Lovers

People once thought that the sauropods lived in lakes, with water to support their great weight. But today scientists think that they must have lived on land, using their long necks to browse on the treetops, as giraffes do. A 40-foot-long neck would have had no use in the water. If the animal had gone into deep water and tried to breathe with its nose at the surface, it would have been unable to do so: the weight of the water on its chest would have been too great for it to breathe in.

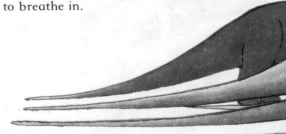

Living Together

Most of the big plant-eating animals that live today move about in herds. Elephants, antelopes, giraffes and kangaroos all travel and feed together. The herd gives them protection. A lion is far more likely to attack a lone animal than a whole herd. Also animals can warn each other of danger. The same thing probably happened in prehistoric times. We know for certain that Iguanodon, a Cretaceous dinosaur, lived in herds. The bones of twenty of them were found all in one place in Belgium. They probably died in a landslide.

Brontosaurus and the other plant-eating dinosaurs probably also formed herds, though the brontosaur herds could not have been very large. Just one Brontosaurus would have eaten about 1000 pounds of food every day. If very many of them had traveled together, there would have been no plants left.

Brontosaur Babies

As far as we know, all dinosaurs laid eggs. Newly hatched Brontosaurs would have been no more than about a yard long. They would have been too small to travel with a herd, even if their parents' herd had stayed in the place where the eggs were laid. So the young probably spent their early lives hidden among the ferns. As they grew, they would have joined up with other youngsters for safety's sake. If, by chance, their parents' herd had still been in the same area when they were ready to travel, they might have joined their herd. The youngster on page 68 of the story is just big enough to wander with his parents' herd. But it is more likely that he would have stayed a little longer with his brothers and sisters while his parents moved on.

Brontosaurus compared with some other sauropods: Diplodocus was the longest, Brachiosaurus the biggest

Melanorosaurus   Cetiosaurus   Brachiosaurus   Diplodocus   Brontosaurus

Chasmosaurus and Late Cretaceous Montana

Skeleton of Chasmosaurus

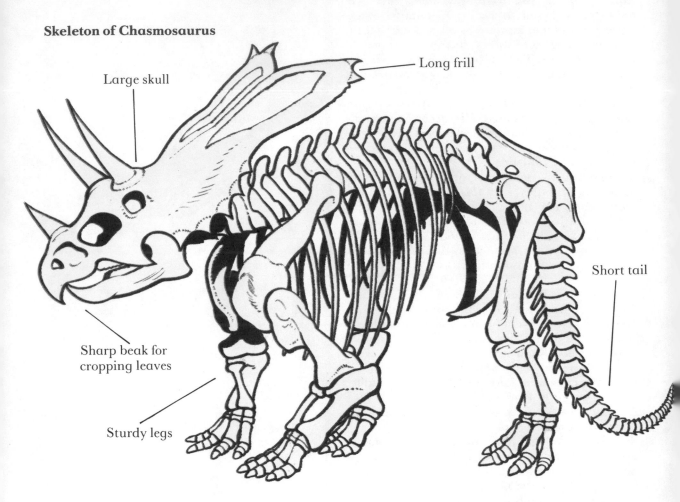

Large skull

Long frill

Sharp beak for cropping leaves

Sturdy legs

Short tail

The time of Chasmosaurus

Scientists have divided the entire history of the world into eras and each era into a number of periods. Between 225 million years ago and 65 million years ago was the Mesozoic Era, the Age of the Dinosaurs. This immense stretch of time has been divided into three periods; the Triassic, the Jurassic and the Cretaceous. The fossils of Chasmosaurus have been found in the most recent rocks of the most recent of these periods, the Cretaceous. This means that it lived about 70 million years ago.

The land of Chasmosaurus

Chasmosaurus fossils have been found in a number of places on the North American continent. They have turned up as far apart as New Mexico and Alberta. The story in the book takes place in what is now Montana about 70 million years ago. All the animals in the story lived in roughly the same place and at the same time as

Chasmosaurus. At that time, Montana, and North America as a whole, was quite different from how it appears today. The Rocky Mountains were only just beginning to be created. They were still fairly low and had not reached the spectacular, snow covered heights which we see today. There is also some evidence to suggest that a shallow, inland sea stretched from the Gulf of Mexico to Hudson Bay, flooding much of what are today the Great Plains, while a broad reach of ocean separated North and South America. Conversely, it is thought that western North America may have been joined to eastern Asia in some way.

Family tree of Chasmosaurus

Chasmosaurus belonged to one of the most distinctive of all dinosaur families. It was a Ceratopsian. The Ceratopsians evolved very late in the Age of the Dinosaurs. The first Ceratopsian was Protoceratops which lived in eastern Asia about 90 million years ago. It was much smaller than Chasmosaurus and had no horns at all. Over the millions of years the line of the Ceratopsians became one of the most numerous and diversified in dinosaur history. There quickly evolved two main lines of evolution; the long frilled Ceratopsians and the short frilled Ceratopsians. Chasmosaurus belonged to the long frilled group, but Styracosaurus, which appears in our story, was a short frilled Ceratopsian. The Ceratopsians continued to evolve and to thrive, producing dozens of species, right up until the end of the Mesozoic Era when they all became extinct. Exactly why such a successful group should die out so completely nobody is really certain.

Other plant-eaters

The late Cretaceous rocks in which the fossils of Chasmosaurus have been found have also yielded many other fossils. Some of the animals whose fossils turn up in rocks of the same age and location have been included in the story, but many others have been found. Alamosaurus, as its name might suggest, was first found in Texas and was named after the famous Alamo. It was a Sauropod and is therefore unusual in that it survived into the late Cretaceous. Most Sauropods, such as Diplodocus and Brontosaurus, had died out millions of years earlier. Parasaurolophus, like Chasmosaurus, belonged to a group which evolved quite late in the Age of the Dinosaurs. It was a Hadrosaur. This group of two legged plant-eaters appeared at about the same time as the Ceratopsians and likewise evolved into many species. Most members of the group are distinguished by the curious growths on their heads. Nobody is really sure what these were used for. Euoplocephalus was one of the commonest dinosaurs from Late Cretaceous Montana and was a close relative of the more famous Ankylosaurus. It had a strong, protective covering of bony armor along the top of its head, body and tail.

Meat-eaters

Many types of carnivorous dinosaurs lived at the same time as Chasmosaurus. Perhaps the most dangerous was Dromaeosaurus. This rather small dinosaur was a very fast runner and agile hunter. Its main weapon was the large, sickle-shaped claw on its hind feet. These were formidable weapons and enabled Dromaeosaurus to bring down large animals, such as Parasaurolophus. The much larger Albertosaurus was a close relative of the famous Tyrannosaurus Rex. Scientists disagree about the role of such large meat-eaters. Some think of them as formidable hunters. Other scientists say that Albertosaurus and its like were too clumsy to hunt as did the Dromaeosaurs and think that such dinosaurs were mere scavengers.

Other Ceratopsians

Triceratops, which lived after Chasmosaurus

Protoceratops, which lived before Chasmosaurus

Dimorphodon and Early Jurassic Europe

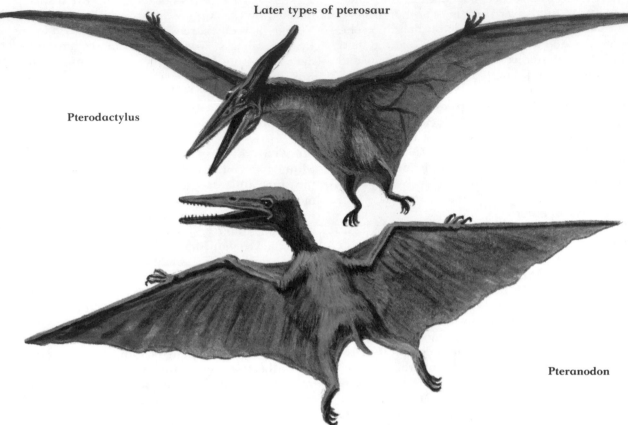

Later types of pterosaur

Pterodactylus

Pteranodon

The days of Dimorphodon

By studying rocks, scientists have been able to divide the entire history of the world into four great eras: the Precambrian, the Paleozoic, the Mesozoic and the Cenozoic. Dimorphodon lived during the fourth period, the Mesozoic which means "middle life". The Mesozoic began about 225 million years ago and ended about 65 million years ago. This great era is itself divided into the three periods, the Triassic, the Jurassic and the Cretaceous. Dimorphodon fossils have been found in the earliest rocks of the Jurassic. This means that the reptile lived about 190 million years ago.

The flying reptiles

Dimorphodon was not a dinosaur. It belonged to a group of reptiles known today as Pterosauria. However, the Pterosauria came under the much larger group of reptiles which is known as the Archosaurs. Archosaur means "ruling reptiles" and it is a very apt name for it is one of the largest of all reptile groups. It includes not only the flying reptiles of millions of years ago but also the crocodiles of today, the extinct Aetosaurs and Phytosaurs and most important of all the dinosaurs. The line which

led to the flying reptiles diverged from the other Archosaurs some time during the Triassic period, that is some 210 million years ago. No fossils have been found of animals which are partly Pterosaur and partly land reptiles. The earliest known fossil is Dimorphodon and this is already a fully developed Pterosaur. However, the later evolution of the Pterosaurs is well recorded by scientists. It is clear that Dimorphodon, with its heavy head and long, bony tail, was a fairly primitive flying reptile. In the course of evolution the Pterosaurs gained smaller heads, which made flying easier, and lost their tails, which meant they could maneuver much more accurately. All the Pterosaurs died out at the end of the Mesozoic, at the same time as the dinosaurs.

The land of Dimorphodon

The fossils of Dimorphodon have been found in England. But 190 million years ago England was very different from today. Perhaps the most noticeable difference would have been the plant life. There were no trees as we know them and no grass at all. Nor were there any flowering plants for they had not yet evolved. The plants which dominated the land were the tall cordates, tree ferns and primitive conifers which can be seen in the story. Other plants included ferns, horsetails, cycads and cycadeoids. Some of these plants can still be found in England, but they are much rarer than they were 190 million years ago, and others have disappeared entirely.

Early Jurassic animals

The time in which Dimorphodon lived was part of the "Age of the Dinosaurs", yet most of the dinosaurs familiar to dinosaur experts had not yet evolved. It was only a few million years earlier that the dinosaurs had first appeared and there had not yet appeared the bewildering variety of creatures with which we are so familiar. Perhaps the best known dinosaur of the period and place was Megalosaurus. This 30 foot long meat eater was one of the first dinosaurs ever to be discovered by scientists. In fact, it was found before anybody knew there had been dinosaurs at all and its bones created quite a sensation. When alive, it was one of the most powerful hunters in the world and must have been a terrifying sight. The Sarcosaurs, which in our story, appear to scavenge from Megalosaurus' kill, were members of the same family of dinosaurs, but were only about 11 feet long. The other hunter in the story, Metriacanthosaurus, was unusual in that it had a row of spines along its back which is thought to have supported a flap of skin. Why Metriacan-

thosaurus needed such a large flap of skin is unclear. Perhaps it was used for display, like the tail of today's peacock, or perhaps it cooled the dinosaur in hot weather. Scelidosaurus was another strange dinosaur. It had strong, bone studs all along its back and sides. These must have given the dinosaur some kind of protection against the attacks of hunters such as Megalosaurus and Metriacanthosaurus. It is possible that the Scelidosaur family evolved into the more famous Stegosaurus many years later. The future belonged to the family of which Ohmdenosaurus was a member; the Sauropods. Though Ohmdenosaurus was only about 13 feet long, later Sauropods would grow to be the largest dinosaurs ever, including the famous Brontosaurus, Diplodocus and Brachiosaurus. There were many other kinds of reptile alive at the time. One of these was the crocodile which was a member of the Archosaur group. The Ichthyosaur, on the other hand, was not an Archosaur. Nobody is really sure how the Ichthyosaur evolved for there are no fossils showing a reptile part way between a land reptile and the Ichthyosaur. However it was a very successful type of reptile and developed into many different species. Today, mammals are the most important type of land animal. Man is a mammal and so are most of the larger land animals, from a mouse to an elephant. During the days of the Dimorphodon, however, mammals were unimportant, and the few species that existed were only about the size of the creature captured by Dimorphodon.

The different structures of a bird's and Dimorphodon's wing

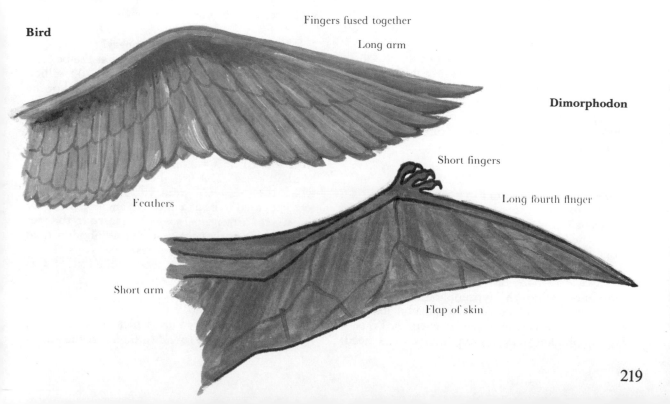

Bird

Fingers fused together

Long arm

Dimorphodon

Short fingers

Long fourth finger

Feathers

Short arm

Flap of skin

Interesting facts about . . .
Hypsilophodon

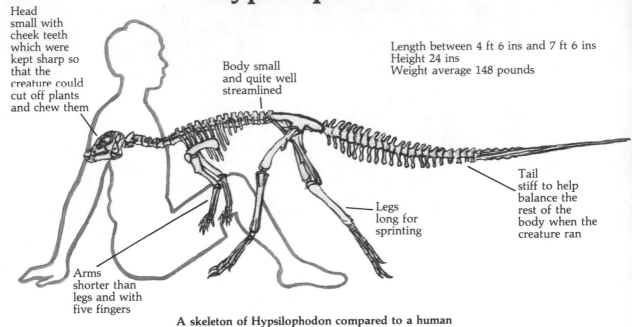

Head small with cheek teeth which were kept sharp so that the creature could cut off plants and chew them

Body small and quite well streamlined

Length between 4 ft 6 ins and 7 ft 6 ins
Height 24 ins
Weight average 148 pounds

Tail stiff to help balance the rest of the body when the creature ran

Legs long for sprinting

Arms shorter than legs and with five fingers

A skeleton of Hypsilophodon compared to a human

Dinosaurs are grouped into two orders. These are the Saurischian dinosaurs and the Ornithischian dinosaurs. Ornithoscian means "bird-hipped". These dinosaurs got their name because their hip bones are arranged like those of birds. The two orders are then divided up into a number of sub-orders. These include the Ornithopods, which means "bird-footed."

Ornithopods were the only group of Ornithischian dinosaurs which could walk or run on their hind legs.

We can compare ornithopods with some animals which live today. Deer take their food in a similar way. They pull leaves off trees. The bird-hipped dinosaurs took food like this.

Hypsilophodon was one of the smaller bird-hipped dinosaurs. In fact Hypsilophodontids didn't weigh as much as an average man (168 pounds).

Bird-hipped Dinosaurs

Hypsilophodon was one of a group of dinosaurs which belonged to a family called Hypsilophodontids. The name Hypsilophodontids means "high ridge teeth". It tells us about the food which the dinosaurs ate.

There were many different kinds of bird-hipped dinosaurs. Although Hypsilophodon was a small dinosaur, it could move very quickly. Its speed helped it to get away from its enemies. When a Hypsilophodon was running quickly its head,

body and tail were all in a straight line. It had to stop sometimes. Then its head was held up in much the same way as a bird holds its head.

One of the fastest creatures

Much work has been carried out on the remains of Hypsilophodons. Although scientists can't be certain, they do believe that it was one of the fastest creatures ever to live on the earth.

When did Hypsilophodon appear?

Hypsilophodon probably appeared at the beginning of the Age of Dinosaurs. This was 200 million years ago. The creature died out at the end of the Age of Dinosaurs, 135 million years later.

Did Hypsilophodon live in trees?

When the remains of the first Hypsilophodons were looked at it was thought that the dinosaur lived in trees. This was because of the way in which the toes were arranged. The largest of the toes appeared to be at a different angle to the other three. This arrangement was compared to the toes of birds. They thought that Hypsilophodon used its toes to hold on to branches.

Later, when more toes were looked at, it was found that they were parallel.

Fast mover on land

Far from being a creature which lived in trees, Hypsilophodon was found to be a fast mover on land. If you look at the skeleton you will see that the bones of the lower leg are very long. All creatures which run quickly have long lower leg bones.

Hypsilophodon's tail was also special. It used its tail for balancing. When the dinosaur was moving quickly its tail kept it stable. Running at fast speeds it also had to avoid obstacles. The tail helped it to turn quickly in all directions.

What did Hypsilophodon eat?

All the bird-hipped dinosaurs ate plants. They all had special teeth. These had ridges on them. It was these ridged teeth which helped Hypsilophodon and the other bird-hipped dinosaurs to crush and grind the seeds and fruits which they ate.

Hypsilophodon had a horny beak. The beak was used to bite off pieces of plants. Inside the beak there was a row of small teeth in the upper part of the mouth. None of the other bird-hipped dinosaurs had small teeth like these. No one has been able to discover their function.

Other bird-hipped Dinosaurs

Some people find it strange that Hypsilophodon and Iguanodon were both bird-hipped dinosaurs. Unlike Hypsilophodon, Iguanodon was very large. It was 16 feet tall and 36 feet long. Whereas Hypsilophodon weighed about 140 pounds, Iguanodon weighed 4.5 tons (9,000 lbs.). You could have put 61 Hypsilophodons inside an Iguanodon!

All three creatures belonged to a group called Ornithopods, which means bird-footed. Iguanodon was large. Large numbers of these creatures have been found. Hypsilophodon was fleet of foot. All three creatures were browsers.

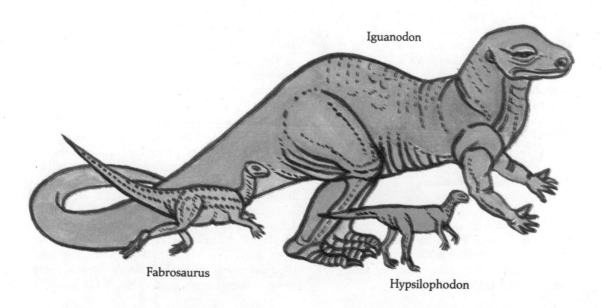

Iguanodon

Fabrosaurus

Hypsilophodon

Interesting facts about . . .
Ichthyosaurus

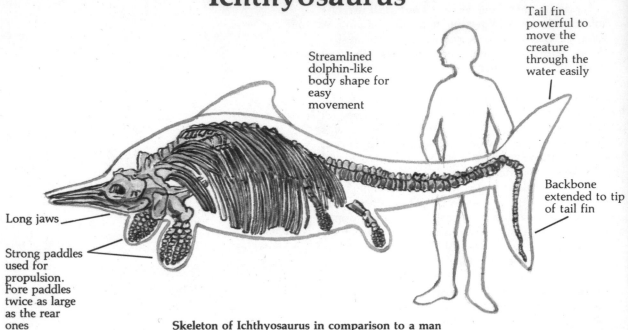

Streamlined dolphin-like body shape for easy movement

Tail fin powerful to move the creature through the water easily

Long jaws

Backbone extended to tip of tail fin

Strong paddles used for propulsion. Fore paddles twice as large as the rear ones

Skeleton of Ichthyosaurus in comparison to a man

What were Ichthyosaurs?

The Ichthyosaurs are known as "fish lizards". They first appeared in the Triassic seas 250 million years ago. So far scientists have not been able to discover where they came from.

The first fish lizard to appear was one called Mixosaurus. It is possible that this particular species developed from reptiles which lived on land. No one is certain. Why a land animal should change its way of life is a mystery.

There were other Ichthyosaurs living in the Triassic period, including one called Cymbospondylus. Ichthyosaurus did not appear until millions of years later in the Jurassic period (195 million years ago to 145 million years ago).

In between the true land animals and the true water animals were other creatures. It is likely that these were like modern amphibians — frogs and toads. Amphibian means "double life". Amphibians have to spend some of their life in the water if they are to survive. By Triassic times the first Ichthyosaur lived completely in the water.

The First Ichthyosaur Remains

The first Ichthyosaur remains were discovered in England at the end of the nineteenth century. A lady named Mary Anning found the first complete Ichthyosaur skeleton. Even before this, some vertebrae (backbones) had been found in 1712. The person who discovered them did not know to what creature they belonged.

Living in Water

Ichthyosaurs were called fish lizards because they had evolved from reptiles, but could swim like fish. Ichthyosaurs were able to move easily through the water because they were streamlined. They also had limbs like large paddles. These helped them swim well. Although all four limbs were paddle-like, the front two were twice as big as the back two. In general shape the Ichthyosaurus was like a dolphin. Some Ichthyosaurs were quite small. There were some 40 inches long. Others were much longer. The longest was about 40 feet in length. Ichthyosaurs had very powerful tail fins which they used to help them move forward. There was also a triangular fin in the middle of the back.

The creature's head was also streamlined. It tapered into a long thin snout similar to a dolphin's.

Preserved Ichthyosaurs

Some complete Ichthyosaur skeletons were found at Holzamaden in Germany. They were so well preserved that scientists could see the outlines of skin in addition to the remains of bones. From these remains scientists were able to see exactly what the paddles and fins were like. These Ichthyosaurs had been so well preserved, the color of the skin could be seen. The remains were in such good condition because when the creatures died they sank to the bottom of the sea. Here they were covered with mud. They were found many millions of years later.

What Did The Ichthyosaurs Eat?

We know what Ichthyosaurs ate because fossil droppings, called coprolites, have been found. These contained the preserved remains of the Ichthyosaurs' food. Some fossil droppings were found near Ichthyosaurs. Others were still inside the bodies of the dead creatures.

Inside the droppings were the remains of a fish called Pholidophorus. These creatures were believed to live close to the surface of the prehistoric seas. From their shape it is also thought that they were fast swimming creatures. Since Pholidophorus were fast swimming fish, Ichthyosaurus must have actively hunted their food. They caught most of it close to the surface of the water.

Other Ichthyosaurs fed on cephalopods. These prehistoric creatures were related to the octopi which live in today's seas. Remains of the cephalopods were found inside the dead Ichthyosaurs. The soft parts of these creatures had been digested. This left large numbers of small, curved, black hooks. These came from the tentacles of the cephalopods.

In the stomach of one young Ichthyosaur 478,000 hooks were found. This juvenile Ichthyosaur was only 60 inches long. It is calculated that this particular creature had eaten about 1,600 cephalopods. Living in the Jurassic seas at the same time as Ichthyosaurus were Plesiosaurs and Pliosaurs. Because all three kinds of marine creature fed on different food, there was no competition.

The illustrations show three creatures which shared the same seas. They fed on different creatures so they did not compete for food.

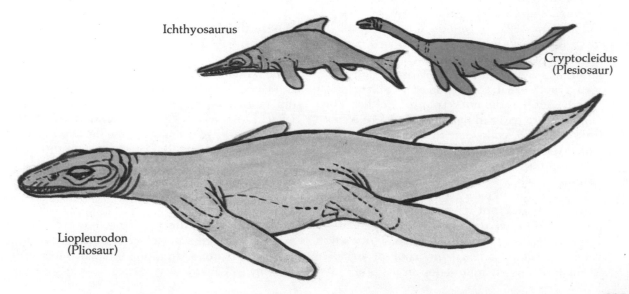

Ichthyosaurus

Cryptocleidus
(Plesiosaur)

Liopleurodon
(Pliosaur)

Iguanodon and Early Cretaceous Europe

Length: 25 feet
Height: 15 feet

Batteries of
crushing teeth

Thumb spike

Bird-like hip (Ornithischia)

Grasping hands

Long legs

Heavy tail to balance body

Skeleton of Iguanodon

"Iguana tooth"

Dinosaurs, like the Iguanodon, lived many millions of years ago. We only know about them today because their bones have been found in ancient rocks. But 150 years ago nobody knew about dinosaurs because their fossils had not been recognized as those of ancient reptiles.

Then, in 1822, a woman found a fossilized tooth in Sussex, England. She showed it to her husband, who was interested in fossil bones. His name was Dr. Mantell. Dr. Mantell had never seen a tooth like it, so he showed it to his scientist friends, but they did not recognize it either. Then one scientist realized that it looked like a tooth from a reptile called an iguana. Dr. Mantell called the prehistoric animal, to which the tooth had belonged, an Iguanodon, which means "iguana tooth".

It was not until many other Iguanodon bones had been found that scientists realized it was a dinosaur. One of the most important finds of Iguanodon fossils was at Maidstone, a town in England. That is why the coat of arms of Maidstone has an Iguanodon in it.

When did Iguanodon live?

Iguanodon lived 130 million years ago at the beginning of the Cretaceous period. This was the last of the periods of the Age of Dinosaurs. The first period was called the Triassic and the middle period was called the Jurassic.

Where did Iguanodon live?

Dr. Mantell found his Iguanodon tooth in Southern England. Other fossils have been found in Belgium and other places in Northern Europe. But when Iguanodon was alive, Europe was very different from today. Stretching across England where London is today, was a range of tall mountains. These are the mountains that you can see on pages 152 and 153. Below the mountains were hills covered in thick forests of conifers and cycads. To the south of the mountains and the forests was a vast lake that covered hundreds of square miles.

In those days the English Channel did not exist and the lake stretched from England right across to Europe. Iguanodon spent most of its time by this lake.

What did Iguanodon eat?

Iguanodon was a large plant-eating dinosaur of the bird-hipped group of dinosaurs. When it stood upright on its hind legs, Iguanodon was about fifteen feet high. This means that it must have been able to reach up into trees and eat the leaves, as you can see on pages 158 and 159. However, the front legs of Iguanodon were quite strong and had small hooves on them. Because of this scientists think that Iguanodon spent much of its time on all four legs browsing on small ferns and cycads.

Iguanodon had no teeth in the front of its mouth, but horny, cutting jaws. It is thought that Iguanodon had a muscular tongue and large cheeks. It would have used its tongue to grasp leaves and foliage, before nipping them off. Iguanodon would then have used its cheeks to move the food across its teeth in the back of the mouth so that it could be properly chewed. These two features would have ensured that Iguanodon was very efficient at eating plants.

Other plant-eaters

The first part of the Cretaceous period, when Iguanodon lived, was very important for the evolution of plant eating dinosaurs. The bird-hipped, or ornithischia dinosaurs were poised to take over from the lizard-hipped plant-eaters.

Throughout the Jurassic period, the lizard-hipped sauropods, such as Brontosaurus, were the most common plant-eating dinosaurs. During the Cretaceous period the ornithischia, like Iguanodon, evolved into many species and became very common. For some reason this only happened in the northern parts of the world. In the south, the sauropods continued to be very common.

The Cetiosauriscus that you can see on page 154 were a type of sauropod that managed to survive in Northern Europe during the Cretaceous.

The diversity of the bird-hipped group of dinosaurs is shown by Hypsilophodon, Polacanthus and Ouranosaurus. Hypsilophodon was a small dinosaur that could run very fast. It ate the leaves and fruits of short plants and could run away from most meat-eaters. Polacanthus was a large, heavy dinosaur that could not move very fast at all. Instead, it used its impressive array of spikes and bony plates to protect itself. Ouranosaurus had a strange crest running down its back, but was otherwise very like Iguanodon. All these dinosaurs were members of the bird-hipped group, so it is not surprising that they managed to take over from the lizard-hipped group of dinosaurs as the most important plant-eaters.

Ouranosaurus, an African relative of Iguanodon which had a 'sail' along its back.

Mamenchisaurus and Late Jurassic China

Skeleton of Mamenchisaurus

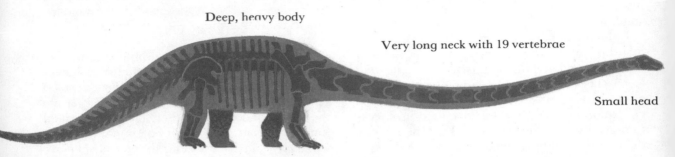

Length: 72 feet
Length of neck: 36 feet

Deep, heavy body

Very long neck with 19 vertebrae

Small head

Long tail

Strong, pillar-like legs to support great weight

Family tree of Mamenchisaurus

Mamenchisaurus belonged to one of the largest and oldest groups of dinosaurs, the sauropods. Sauropods first appeared at the very start of the Jurassic period and survived right through to the end of the Age of Dinosaurs. All sauropods shared similar characteristics: they were all large, all had long necks, all had long tails and they were all plant eaters. At about 72 feet long, Mamenchisaurus was one of the largest sauropods. It certainly had the longest neck of any known dinosaur, with 19 neck vertebrae. The sauropods belonged to the saurischia, or lizard-hipped, group of dinosaurs. All the meat-eating dinosaurs and a small group of dinosaurs called the prosauropods belonged to this category. All other dinosaurs had a bird-like hip and so are known as ornithischia. After the time of Mamenchisaurus, the ornithischia became increasingly important as plant–eaters and sauropods became rarer and smaller.

The world of Mamenchisaurus

In the time of Mamenchisaurus, China, like the world as a whole, was very different from how it is today. All the continents were in different positions on the globe and many oceans did not exist. This meant that most of the land was joined together into one large continent across which animals could roam freely. The plant life of the period was also very different. There were no flowers and no grass, nor were there many other plants which we would recognize today. Among the strange plants of that time were cycads, giant ferns, Williamsonias and many different species of horsetails. There were the familiar conifer trees and small ferns which continue to exist to this day.

In the animal world in those days, birds and mammals were unimportant compared with their position today. Mammals had evolved many millions of years earlier, but they were still small, insignificant animals. Birds had only recently appeared and were probably clumsy fliers which could not compete with the reptilian pterosaurs which filled the skies. The land really belonged to the dinosaurs. Most of the animals encountered by Mamenchisaurus in the story were dinosaurs which lived in China at that time. Gongubusaurus was a small bird-hipped dinosaur which ate low-growing vegetation and could run quickly. Yangchuanosaurus was a large, powerful dinosaur whose large claws and sharp teeth tell scientists that this was a ferocious hunter, probably quite capable of killing and eating a Mamenchisaurus. It was about 33 feet long and was related to the more famous Allosaurus. As can be guessed from its appearance, Tuojiangosaurus belonged to the same family as the well known Stegosaurus which was living in North America at that time. Tuojiangosaurus was another bird-hipped dinosaur, like Gongubusaurus. Mamenchisaurus was not the only sauropod to live in China at this time. It had to compete for food with Zigongosaurus which was named after the place where its fossils have been found. One of the smallest dinosaurs of the time was Sinocoelurus, whose name means "Chinese hollow-tail". Scientists have found only four teeth from this animal. No bones have ever been found. Since the teeth are very similar to those of a dinosaur then living in America, scientists can be reasonably sure of what Sinocoelurus looked like and how it lived.

When did Mamenchisaurus live?

Mamenchisaurus lived during the Age of the Dinosaurs. Scientists call this stretch of time the Mesozoic Era, which means "Middle Life". This era has been divided into three periods. First, the Triassic, which began about 225 million years ago and lasted for 35 million years. Second, the Jurassic, which began 190 million years ago and ended about 136 million years ago. The Final period is called the Cretaceous, and it ended some 65 million years ago. Mamenchisaurus fossils have been found in the most recent Jurassic rocks. This means that it lived about 140 million years ago.

Home of Mamenchisaurus

The fossils of Mamenchisaurus were found by scientists near to the town of Mamenchi in China. The dinosaur gained its name, which means "lizard from Mamenchi", because it was found near that town. Mamenchisaurus belonged to a group of dinosaurs known as diplodocids. It is unusual to have a diplodocid from Asia. Most diplodocids came from America, Europe or Africa.

The life of Mamenchisaurus

Mamenchisaurus became extinct many millions of years before the first man walked on earth. This means that there are no records of any human having ever seen a Mamenchisaurus. However, scientists can discover much about a dinosaur from its bones and teeth and can guess at how it lived. Mamenchisaurus had no natural weapons with which to attack other animals and its teeth were simple and peg-like. This means that it ate plants. Its enormous size and long neck indicate which sort of plants it ate. Mamenchisaurus probably used its long neck to reach high into the trees for food other dinosaurs were too short to eat. The strong legs and relatively small feet indicate that Mamenchisaurus walked on hard, dry ground. It did not spend much time in swamps. Danger sometimes theatened in the shape of fierce, meat-eating dinosaurs. At times like that, Mamenchisaurus would bunch together and lash out their tails. Because of its large size and small mouth Mamenchisaurus probably had to spend most of its time eating in order to survive.

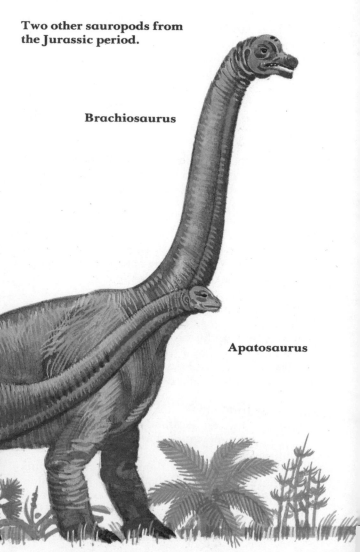

Two other sauropods from the Jurassic period.

Brachiosaurus

Apatosaurus

227

Triceratops and the Cretaceous World

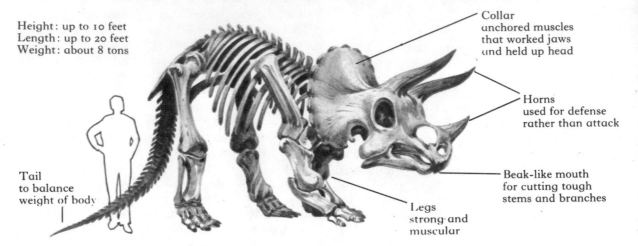

Height: up to 10 feet
Length: up to 20 feet
Weight: about 8 tons

Collar
unchored muscles
that worked jaws
and held up head

Horns
used for defense
rather than attack

Tail
to balance
weight of body

Beak-like mouth
for cutting tough
stems and branches

Legs
strong and
muscular

The skeleton of Triceratops compared in size with a man

When did Triceratops live?

Triceratops lived during the Mesozoic Era, or Age of Dinosaurs. The Mesozoic Era began 225 million years ago and lasted for about 160 million years. Scientists divide the era into three periods: the Triassic, Jurassic and Cretaceous. Triceratops lived during the last one, the Cretaceous.

What kind of dinosaur was Triceratops?

Triceratops belonged to a group of plant-eating dinosaurs called horned dinosaurs, or ceratopsians. The first ceratopsians were small creatures with little armor. But later ones like Triceratops were big and strong with dangerous horns and spikes. They were rather like reptilian rhinoceroses. The picture on the next page shows some of the different types.

Hot or Cold Blood?

The ceratopsians, like all the dinosaurs and many other prehistoric animals, were reptiles. The reptiles we know today, such as lizards and snakes, are cold-blooded creatures. They are as warm or as cold as the air around them. They cannot move about if the air is too cold. Birds and mammals are warm-blooded. They have fur, hair or feathers to keep them warm and their temperature does not change. They can live anywhere.

Many scientists now think that the dinosaurs may have been warm-blooded even though they were reptiles. They may have had hair and been able to move about much faster than modern reptiles can. But nobody knows for certain.

Reptiles and Their Young

In the story, Triceratops laid her eggs in a sand nest and then left them to hatch by themselves. Modern turtles and most other reptiles do the same. Scientists have found nests of fossilized eggs belonging to a ceratopsian dinosaur called Protoceratops. So it is most likely that Triceratops also laid eggs.

What did Triceratops eat?

We know how Triceratops ate from the shape of its teeth and jaws. It plucked or snapped off the branches of plants with its parrot-like beak. Then it sliced up the tough leaves and stems with its teeth. These had sharp edges and moved across each other like scissor blades. In fact, they were more like a meat-eater's teeth than a plant-eater's.

To move its huge jaws, Triceratops had long, strong muscles. The muscles were attached to the bony frill around its neck. The frill also helped Triceratops to hold up its enormous head, which reached 8 feet in length.

Plants of the Cretaceous

The plants that Triceratops ate and sheltered beneath were probably quite different from the ones we know today. A Cretaceous forest would have had lots of big ferns, conifers, palms, and plants called cycads (Ornithomimus is hiding behind a cycad on page 193). But there would not have been many of the trees with flowers and fruits that we see in our woods today.

Before the Cretaceous period there were almost no flowering plants at all. And even during the Cretaceous there were not many different kinds. One of the first flowering plants was the magnolia (see page204). It was a long time before there was any grass. The ground must have been covered by moss or ferns.

Animals of the Cretaceous

Today the biggest and most important animals are mammals. But, during the Cretaceous, mammals were only the size of mice, almost too small for the mighty dinosaurs to notice. (You can see a mammal on page193 and on several later pages.)

The fiercest of the dinosaurs were meat-eaters such as Tyrannosaurus (see page197). Almost no creature was safe from its cruel teeth. Some animals, like Ornithomimus, could escape from it by running or hiding. Others had to rely on their strength or armor. Triceratops was only just tough enough to withstand an attack; a weaker animal, either older or younger, would probably have been killed. Ankylosaurus could fight off attackers with its big clubbed tail or sink down on its stomach and rely on its bony armor, as it did on page200.

The oddest of all the animals in the story were the Stegoceras dinosaurs (see pages 18 & 19), sometimes called boneheads. Their skulls had as much as 10 inches of bone on them. They may have fought with other animals, or with each other over a female, perhaps, as deer do today. Their "crash helmets" would have stopped them bashing out each other's brains.

We know that there must have been many birds in the Cretaceous, although not many remains of them have been found. There were also great flying reptiles called pterosaurs (see page199). They had light, leathery wings like bats, and could glide, though they could not fly like birds. They lived mostly on fish which they snatched from the water in their long beaks. Most of the other creatures in this book, crocodiles, insects and so on, have close relatives living today, so we know more about them.

Some ceratopsian, or horned, dinosaurs

Protoceratops   Monoclonius   Styracosaurus   Triceratops

Glossary

ALAMOSAURUS [AL-a-mo-SAW-rus] This long-necked herbivore fed on tree tops. Its fossils were found in Texas, and it was named after the famous Alamo. *See page 84.*

ALBERTOSAURUS [al-BUR-toe-SAW-rus] This fierce carnivore, named because its first fossil was discovered in Alberta, Canada, was a close relative of TYRANNOSAURUS REX, and was considered another "King of the Jungle." *See page 81.*

ALLOSAURUS [AL-oh-SAW-rus] Its name means "different reptile." This carnivore grew to 40 feet in length and weighed up to 2 tons. It had a large head and blade-like fangs. This ferocious beast walked upright and hunted in packs. *See Chapter One; pages 59,210-211.*

Brontosaurus

ANKYLOSAURUS [ANK-ee-lo-SAW-rus] Its name means "stiff reptile." This herbivore had tough, bony armor and a spiked tail for defense. It had to spend the whole day eating in order to satisfy its hunger. *See page 200.*

APATOSAURUS [a-PAT-oh-SAW-rus] Its name means "deceptive reptile." Another name for BRONTOSAURUS. *See page 50,227.*

ARCHAEOPTERYX [AR-kee-OP-ter-ricks] Its name means "ancient wing." This narrow-beaked, winged reptile (Pterosaur) was the earliest known bird. It ate both insects and meat, and was about 14 inches long. *See Chapter Two; pages 14,18,212-213.*

Allosaurus

BRACHIOSAURUS [BRAK-ee-oh-SAW-rus] Its name means "arm lizard." This herbivore was the largest of all dinosaurs: up to 90 feet long, 40 feet high, and weighing 100 tons. Its long neck enabled it to reach food in high tree tops. *See page 70,227.*

BRONTOSAURUS [BRON-toe-SAW-rus] Its name means "thunder lizard." Also known as APATOSAURUS. This herbivore had a small head and peg-like teeth. It weighed 30 tons, lived in herds on dry land, and ate about 1000 lbs. of food per day. *See Chapter Three; page 16,214-215.*

CAMPTOSAURUS [KAMP-toe-SAW-rus] Its name means "bent reptile." This herbivore had a bird-like, horny beak. It was 16 feet long, weighed 1/2 ton, and could stand on its hind legs to reach for food, although it walked on all fours. *See page 48.*

Diplodocus

CERATOSAURUS [ser-RAT-oh-SAW-rus] This ferocious carnivore was a fierce hunter. It grew approximately 15-20 feet in length and had a peculiar horn on the top of its snout. *See page 211.*

CETIOSAURUS [SEE-tee-oh-SAW-rus] Its name means "whale lizard." This herbivore weighed as much as three elephants, and measured 60 feet from head to tail. It had dull little teeth, like most other plant-eaters. *See page 154.*

CHASMOSAURUS [KAZ-moh-SAW-rus] Its name means "ravine reptile." This sharp-beaked herbivore had a small nasal horn and two big horns that jutted out from its brow. It had a short tail, button-like scales, and a large spiked collar. *See Chapter Four;pages 216-217.*

Tyrannosaurus

COMPSOGNATHUS [KOMP-so-NAY-thus] Its name means "pretty jaw." This small carnivore resembled a wingless bird. It fed on large insects and small lizards. *See page 45.*

CYMBOSPONDYLUS [SIM-bus-POND-ee-lus] This fish-eater was related to the ICHTHYOSAURUS, and had a long neck and flippers. *See page 222.*

DEINONYCHUS [dye-NONN-ee-kus] Its name means "terrible claw." This small carnivore was 9 feet long and 3 feet high. It had a long tail for balancing, could run very fast, and hunted in packs. *See page 31.*

DILOPHOSAURUS [dye-LO-fo-SAW-rus] This large and powerful carnivore was about 20 feet long, and had a pair of bony crests on its head. *See page 70.*

Nothosaurus

DIMETRODON [dye-MET-tro-don] Its name means "two-sized tooth." This carnivore measured 10 feet long, and had a "sail" on its back supported by spikes. It is believed that the sail may have worked like a radiator, helping the dinosaur to control its body temperature. *See page 30.*

Euoplocephalus

DIMORPHODON [dye-MORF-oh-don] Its name means "two-formed tooth." This winged carnivore had a blunt, short, heavy head armed with teeth, and a long bony tail and wings. *See Chapter Five; page 70,218-219.*

DIPLODOCUS [DIP-lo-DOE-kus] Its name means "double beam." This leathery-skinned herbivore was the world's largest land animal, measuring 91 feet in length, with a whip-like tail measuring 45 feet. *See pages 10,16.*

Alamosaurus

DROMAEOSAURUS [DROM-ee-uh-SAW-rus] This small, but fierce, bird-like carnivore was about the size of a grown human. A fast runner, it hunted in packs, and leaped on its prey with large, sickle-shaped claws. *See page 76.*

Mamenchisaurus

DRYOSAURUS [DRY-oh-SAW-rus] Its name means "wood reptile." This small herbivore was about 6-1/2 feet long. It was a fast runner, and fought by kicking with its small, powerful legs. *See page 43.*

Pteranodon

ELAPHROSAURUS [el-AFF-row-SAW-rus] This ostrich-like fish-eater grew up to 20 feet in length. *See page 42.*
EUOPLOCEPHALUS [you-OP-loe-KEFF-a-lus] Its name means "well-armored head." This heavily-armored herbivore weighed 4-5 tons, and was 20 feet long. Its tail ended in a large round club that was used as defensive weapon. *See page 89.*

Iguanodons

GONGUBUSAURUS [GONG-you-bus-SAW-rus] This small, bird-hipped herbivore ate low-growing vegetation, and could run very fast. *See page 177.*

GONIOPHOLIS [GONE-ee-oh-FOE-les] This herbivore used the water to keep its body cool during the midday heat. *See page 157*

HYPSILOPHODON [HIP-sill-oh-foe-DON] Its name means "high-ridge teeth." This small, horny-beaked herbivore was one of the fastest creatures ever to live on Earth. It was 4-7 feet long, 2 feet tall, and it weighed 150 lbs. *See Chapter Six; pages 11,155,220-221.*

Plateosaurus

ICHTHYOSAURUS [IK-thee-oh-SAW-rus] Its name means "fish reptile." This air-breathing fish-eater resembled the dolphin and measured 33 feet long. It was a powerful swimmer and never left the water. *See Chapter Seven; pages 11,101,222,223.*

IGUANODON [ee-GWON-oh-don] Its name means "iguana tooth." This two-footed herbivore had a "thumb" that acted like a bony spike. This spike was used as a defensive weapon, and sometimes grew to 10 inches in length. *See Chapter Eight; pages 30,116,123, 221,224-225.*

LYSTROSAURUS [LIE-stro-SAW-rus] This mammal-like herbivore lived a semi-aquatic existence, similar to today's hippo. *See page 70.*

MAMENCHISAURUS [ma-MEN-che-SAW-rus] Its name means "lizard from Mamenchi." Named for the town in China where its fossils were found, this small-headed herbivore had the longest neck of any dinosaur, reaching up to 36 feet in length. *See Chapter Nine; page 71, 226-227.*

Stegoceras

METRIACANTHOSAURUS [MET-tree-a-CAN-tho-SAW-rus] This carnivore had a row of spikes along its back which supported a flap of skin used for heating and cooling. *See page 103.*

MIXOSAURUS [MIS-oh-SAW-rus] Its name means "half reptile." This fish-eater was the first fish lizard to appear. *See page 222.*

Gongubusaurus

MONOCLONIUS [MON-oh-KLONE-ee-us] This frilled herbivore had a single horn, and could run quite fast for a reptile. *See page 229.*

Archaeopteryx

MEGALOSAURUS [MEG-a-low-SAW-rus] Its name means "great reptile." This large carnivore was one of the first dinosaurs to be discovered. It grew to 30 feet in length. *See pages 39,92,116,129,152,161.*

NOTHOSAURUS [NO-tho-SAW-rus] This marine reptile ranged from 1.5 feet to 20 feet in length, and had a back fin and webbed feet. *See page 31.*

OHMDENOSAURUS [ome-DEN-oh-SAW-rus] This long-necked herbivore was a relative of the BRONTOSAURUS and the DIPLODOCUS. *See page 103.*

PARASAUROLOPHUS [PAR-a-saw-ROW-low-fus] Its name means "rather like a ridged reptile." This duck-billed herbivore had an elaborate head crest which was used to enhance its sense of smell. *See page 80.*

Brachiosaurus

Ichthyosaurus

ORNITHOLESTES [or-nith-oh-LESS-teez] This scavenging carnivore ate birds and their eggs. It was very fast and nimble, and roughly 6 feet long. *See page 29,55.*

ORNITHOMIMUS [OR-nith-oh-MEE-mus] Its name means "bird imitator." This toothless creature had a horny bill, long, slender back legs, a long neck and tail, and a small head. It was one of the fastest dinosaurs. *See page 192.*

PELOROSAURUS (pe-LOR-oh-SAW-rus] This long-necked herbivore measured approximately 50 feet in length. *See page 38.*

Protoceratops

Albertosaurus

OURANOSAURUS [oo-RAN-oh-SAW-rus] Its name means "valiant monitor lizard." This herbivore, who was an African relative of the IGUANODON, had a "sail" along its back for temperature regulation. *See page 225.*

PLATEOSAURUS [PLAT-ee-oh-SAW-rus] Its name means "flat reptile." Some scientists believe that this herbivore was the first warm-blooded dinosaur. *See page 71.*

PLESIOSAURUS [PLEE-see-oh-SAW-rus] This fish-eating marine reptile laid its eggs on land. It propelled itself through the water with powerful, paddle-shaped limbs. *See page 31.*

POLACANTHUS [POL-a-KAN-thus] A medium-sized herbivore, resembling a giant armadillo. This armored dinosaur had many spikes and bony plates for protection. *See pages 118,167.*

PROTOCERATOPS [PRO-toe-SERR-a-tops] Its name means "first horned face." This heavily-built herbivore was the first dinosaur to have a shield over its neck, and a horn on its head. *See page 71,229.*

Triceratops

PTERANODON [ter-ANN-oh-don] Its name means "winged and toothless." This leathery-winged, fish-eating Pterosaur (*not* a dinosaur) rode the wind currents, and carried food in its beak. *See pages 10,122.*

PTERODACTYLUS [TERR-oh-DACK-til-us] Its name means "finger wing." This was the smallest of the winged reptiles or Pterosaurs. It had a short tail, a horny beak, and long wing bones. *See page 140.*

RHAMPHORHYNCHUS [RAM-foe-RINK-us] Its name means "beak snout." This carnivorous, winged reptile or Pterosaur had broad wings, and resembled a crow with a long tail. *See page 30.*

SCELIDOSAURUS [skel-LY-doh-SAW-rus] Its name means "limb reptile." This four-legged, bony-plated herbivore had studs along its back and tail for protection. *See page 92.*

Hysilophodon

SINOCOELURUS [SIGN-oh-koe-LEW-rus] Its name means "Chinese hollow-tail." Scientists have found only four teeth, but no bones, from this small carnivore. *See page 186.*

STEGOCERAS [steg-GOSS-er-rus] Its name means "roof horn." This small, bone-headed dinosaur was no taller than a grown human. *See page 206.*

STEGOSAURUS [STEG-oh-SAW-rus]

Its name means "roof reptile." This platebacked herbivore had bony spikes that projected sideways from its tail. It was one of the first dinosaurs to become extinct. *See pages 16,54.*

Dilophosaurus

Chasmosaurus

STYRACOSAURUS [sty-RACK-oh-SAW-rus]

Its name means "spiny reptile." This large-headed herbivore had a long nasal horn and an elaborately frilled collar of spikes. *See page 83,229.*

TEINUROSAURUS [TIE-new-row-SAW-rus]

This small carnivore was a fast runner and a dangerous hunter. *See page 46.*

TRICERATOPS [try-SERR-a-tops]

Its name means "three-horned face." This herbivore resembled a huge rhino. Its nasal horn was short, but a pair of 3-foot long horns projected from its brow. These horns were used for defense, not attack. *See Chapter Ten;pages 228-229.*

TUOJIANGOSAURUS [TWO-oh-JANG-oh-SAW-rus]

Named for the town in China in which its bones were first found, this armor-plated herbivore belonged to the same family as the STEGOSAURUS. *See page 183.*

TYRANNOSAURUS REX [tie-RAN-oh-SAW-rus recks]

Its name means "tyrant reptile." The largest carnivore ever to walk the earth, this 50-foot long, 20-foot high king of the meat-eaters weighed 7 tons. *See pages 196,211.*

YANGCHUANOSAURUS [YANG-chew-AN-oh-SAW-rus]

The bones of this ferocious carnivore were found near Yangchun, in China. It hunted in packs, and measured 33 feet in length. *See page 179.*

ZIGONGOSAURUS [ze-GONG-oh-SAW-rus]

This very large, long-necked herbivore was named after the city of Zingong, in China. *See page 185.*